Modeling Fiscal Policy in the European Union

Polish Studies in Economics

Edited by Ryszard Kokoszczyński

Volume 5

PL ACADEMIC RESEARCH

Janusz Kudła / Konrad Walczyk / Robert Kruszewski /
Katarzyna Kopczewska / Agata Kocia

Modeling Fiscal Policy in the European Union

PL ACADEMIC RESEARCH

Bibliographic Information published by the Deutsche Nationalbibliothek
The Deutsche Nationalbibliothek lists this publication in the Deutsche Nationalbibliografie; detailed bibliographic data is available in the internet at http://dnb.d-nb.de.

Library of Congress Cataloging-in-Publication Data
Kudła, Janusz.
Modeling fiscal policy in the European Union / Janusz Kudła, Konrad Walczyk, Robert Kruszewski, Katarzyna Kopczewska, Agata Kocia. — 1 Edition.
pages cm. — (Polish studies in economics ; v. 5)
Includes bibliographical references.
ISBN 978-3-631-65830-7 (Print : alk. paper) — ISBN 978-3-653-05004-2 (E-Book) 1. Fiscal policy—European Union countries. 2. Taxation—European Union countries. 3. Taxation—Econometric models. I. Walczyk, Konrad, 1973- II. Title.
HJ1000.K83 2015
339.5'2094—dc23
2015007145

The publication is financed by Polish National Science Centre as a research project number 2011/03/B/HS4/05552.

Cover Design:
© Olaf Gloeckler, Atelier Platen, Friedberg

ISSN 2191-8848
ISBN 978-3-631-65830-7 (Print)
E-ISBN 978-3-653-05004-2 (E-Book)
DOI 10.3726/978-3-653-05004-2

PL Academic Research is an Imprint of Peter Lang GmbH.

Peter Lang – Frankfurt am Main · Bern · Bruxelles · New York · Oxford · Warszawa · Wien

This publication has been peer reviewed.

www.peterlang.com

Contents

Introduction

The idea for this book has originated in the light of the ongoing debate on whether taxes should be harmonized in the European Union and, if so, to what degree. The discussion has been sparked further because of two reasons: firstly, because of the economic crisis and secondly, because of the impact of countries indebtedness. Debt crises in the European Union countries raise a question: what is the transfer mechanism between various economic phenomena – tax revenues, spending and debt. In all European Union countries public borrowing is necessary to supplement inefficient public revenue in order to provide the level of public goods and services required by its citizens. This need arises also when tax revenues decrease while the level of public goods and services remains roughly constant. Furthermore, obtaining the tax revenues from capital, labor and consumption a government can optimize the tax mix, in order to obtain the maximum budget revenue. However, in practice the tax mix is a result of not only economic optimization but also of public bargaining. This is why the analysis presented in this book has to include public debt with the tax mix optimization.

The purpose of this study is to derive some analytical economic models that will allow for the assessment of the consequences implied by various forms of fiscal integration in the short and long term. We especially focus on propositions postulated to implementation in European Union. It is our hope that undertaken study helps to explain the causes of existing discrepancies in the literature about the desired direction of fiscal policy integration at European Union level, including the impact of international tax competition specificity. While the earlier models of international tax competition theory pointed out the need for close harmonization of direct taxation – unifying their structure and rates (according to the previously conducted harmonization of indirect taxes) – the new ones, especially generated by new economic geography and extended models of traditional tax competition, undermine legitimacy of such a integration and even question it. It should be stressed that both mentioned streams of economic theory are relatively new and have not been unified yet, which indicates the potential benefits from the synergy of combining these two ideas into one new model. Therefore the conducted research could be useful for the further development of the tax competition theory as well as for altering the existing fiscal policy.

Considering the reviewed contemporary theories of the tax system design and existing empirical research (presented in Chapter 1), the tax competition static model with three tax rates and bonds issuance will be developed (in Chapter 2). The constructed analytical model, involving the equilibrium of tax rates between two countries, helps to investigate the impact of some important augmentations, such as the inclusion of agglomeration effect and the concept of fiscal solvency to the fiscal policy under international tax competition pressure. The fiscal solvency hypothesis is an extension of the theory of international tax competition related to the issue of sovereign debt and to the long-term credibility, whereas the agglomeration effect consists of the increasing productivity of capital gathered in neighboring localization. The basic static model analyses the direct economic impact of such policies as the harmonization of capital income tax base with formula apportionment and the imposition of transaction tax on income from financial transaction with government (bonds issuance).

We also strive to develop (in Chapter 3) the dynamic model of fiscal policy including three tax rates and bond issuance but with a slightly different objective function. It should allow for prediction of tax rates behavior in the long term when the purpose of government is to maximize fiscal revenues instead of maximization of representative consumer utility. These two models together shed some light on the confusion about the desired scope of fiscal integration in European Union.

Subsequently in Chapter 4, the relation between taxation and debt will be verified econometrically using regression of panel data and spatial econometrics methods. The data used should cover a longer period from 2002 to 2011. In addition, we are going to verify the predictions of derived models with econometric methods. The final result of the study is to identify the best options for fiscal reform at the EU level that could be recommended for political implementation in Chapter 5. Finally we will try to formulate some possible consequences of various kinds of fiscal integration, taking into account the predictions of our model. Special emphasis will be put on the proposals of tax and fiscal policy reform at European Union level.

Reliable models of fiscal competition can improve analysis of fiscal reform performed in the European Union. Eventually, it should prevent the recurrence of similar crisis in the future. The last statement seems very important for Europe's development and the well-being of its residents. Recommendation formulated on the basis of the model can be used indirectly by the EU authorities and fiscal policy makers. These conclusions may be very important for Poland which is now considering an entry into the Eurozone. This entry will inevitably change the mechanisms Poland can use to adjust to economic shocks. It should be stressed that general structure of analysis does not preclude its usefulness in determining the assumptions and details of fiscal reforms in countries not intending to participate in monetary union. Formulating such a model can surely help to understand the transmission mechanism of debt crisis in applying it to recent debt crisis of southern European countries, while also helping to avoid future mistakes of public policy.

Chapter 1
Taxation and debt in European countries

1. Tax systems in theory

In general, a government can raise revenues by taxation, borrowing or printing money, or charging for goods and services it provides. If we exclude the latter two options from consideration, the first two government financing alternatives[1] are equivalent as long as they do not make an individual's behavior dependent on the form of finance used. Economic agents are not, however, indifferent to the means by which a government covers its expenditure because various types of taxes affect the two, statically separate to each other, allocation decisions – how much to work (or spend time for leisure) and consume (or save). Instead, then, of draining any specific market (for labor, capital or consumption goods) 'to the bottom', a government diversifies funding sources. By doing this it achieves two goals simultaneously: it minimizes the welfare loss as a tax rate on a broader tax base can be lower, and prevents tax avoidance by substituting taxed by untaxed activities. If government spending is given, raising revenues from one source makes it possible to lower receipts from another. In this sense, the forms of finance a government uses are interrelated, or, in other words, they compose together a tax structure or a tax-mix – a system of related components, each measured by its share in total revenues.

The problem of the design of the tax structure is differently viewed in economic theory, depending on the perspective taken.

1.1. Optimal taxation

Since the pioneering works of Mirrlees (1971), Judd (1985) and Chamley (1986) the traditional models of optimal taxation, that assume social welfare to be maximized subject to some constraints, basically suggest that, in an open economy, consumption and labor income should be taxed instead of capital income (see

1 It is unrealistic for a government to rely solely on the borrowing. Due to scarce productive resources and their diminishing marginal productivity it would ultimately end up with taxing people. We might then think of government debt as a specific form of taxation. As Rosen (2008, p. 473) puts it aptly, 'the choice between tax and debt finance is just a choice between the timing of the taxes'.

Chari and Kehoe, 1999; Gordon, 2000; Auerbach and Hines, 2002; or Mankiw, Weinzierl and Yagan, 2009 for reviews of the literature). The reason is that the supply of capital is very responsive to capital taxes which discourage saving and, in the result, negatively affect future output of an economy. Incidentally, by the similar reasoning it is claimed that intermediate goods, which are input to production, should be exempted from taxes (Diamond and Mirrlees, 1971). Consistently with these propositions, value-added and labor taxes constitute main sources of government revenues in the developed countries[2]. And if, instead of economic efficiency, equity is a primary policy concern, governments should particularly use income taxes (Atkinson and Stiglitz, 1980).

There are, however, few exceptions to the principle of zero capital taxation. If individuals face idiosyncratic, uninsured income shocks, they may precautionarily over-save, and a tax on capital income would be preventive (Aiyagari, 1994). Or, alternatively, a government may use it for redistribution purposes when agents are heterogeneous in their abilities to earn income (Conesa, Kitao and Krueger, 2009). Using a capital tax as a corrective device is also advisable when various labor market imperfections exist. Richter and Schneider (2001) find that a positive tax on capital is optimal when:

- there are institutional constraints limiting taxation of profits earned by households (see also Eggert and Goerke, 2004);
- the labor market is a monopsony (labor and capital are not substitutable);
- the labor market is oligopolistic and the unions set wages above the equilibrium level (see also Koskela and Schöb, 2002);
- there are unemployment benefits tied to gross salaries.

This strand of optimal taxation literature highly stresses the optimal tax-mix depends critically on the level of substitutability between capital and labor. The high substitutability promotes capital taxation whereas the complementarity favors a tax on labor.

The latest works on optimal taxation (e.g. Golosov, Kocherlakota and Tsyvinsky, 2003; Albanesi and Sleet, 2006; Golosov, Tsyvinsky and Werning, 2006) consider another link between labor and capital that affect interactions between the two types of taxes. The basic idea is that individuals respond to taxes not only in the time they are imposed but also in preceding and succeeding periods. In a hypothetic world with no taxes they would tend to smooth their consumption over the lifetime by saving when they earn more and dis-saving otherwise. Labor

2 The next subsection discusses this in more detail.

taxes may distort the intertemporal choice by providing incentives to work less or accumulate more. Hence, there is a place for a capital tax to correct these distortions.

Finally, Piketty and Saez (2013) show that, under capital market imperfections and uncertainty, the question whether the optimal tax-mix between labor and capital taxation includes a positive capital income tax is a matter of the intertemporal elasticity of substitution. They generally conclude that the traditional models of optimal taxation are built on too restrictive assumptions and might therefore be misleading. One way for further research is to expand the models with the possibility that countries fiscally compete/cooperate with others.

1.2. International tax competition

The standard tax competition literature points out primarily negative aspects of tax competition among closely connected nation-states, leading to the so-called race-to-the-bottom that lowers revenues collected for national budgets (Zodrow and Mieszkowski, 1986). The mechanism is as follows: by lowering capital taxes, countries reduce tax burden on the most mobile factor of production, i.e. one which can easily be attracted from other countries. However, since tax rates decline, revenues also decrease and so does the provision of public goods. In order to avoid this spiraling effect, countries may agree to harmonize taxes at the level accurate to secure the supply of public goods. Such models were developed both theoretically and then empirically tested in the late 1990s and early 2000s (e.g. Bucovetsky and Wilson, 1991; Wilson, 1999; Wilson and Wildasin, 2004; Krogstrup, 2004). Although the basic assumptions of the model were modified by introducing: heterogeneous economies (Bucovetsky, 1991; Wilson, 1991), more complex tax structures (Gordon and Wilson, 2001; Gordon and Hines, 2002), or maximization of tax revenues as the government's objective (Edwards and Keen, 1996), the general conclusion that labor should be taxed heavier than capital has not changed (see Genschel and Schwarz, 2011 for a survey of the literature). Empirical studies have not given a clear-cut answer, confirming (Winner, 2005; Bénassy-Quéré, Gobalraja & Trannoy, 2007) or denying (Garrett & Mitchell, 2001; Swank, 1998) the theoretical proposition. Further developments of the basic model have led to the formulation of a number of alternative hypotheses answering the challenges of empirical research:

- easing fiscal instability in a result of opening of economies and globalization of business activity, with an increase in public spending and consequently – in order to cover them – an increase in taxes (Swank, 1998; Garrett & Mitchell, 2001);

- higher tax burden on non-residents in comparison to residents (Huizinga & Nielsen, 1997; Eijffinger & Wagner, 2002; Sørensen, 2000);
- heterogeneity of capital resulting in that the tax competition applies only to (more) mobile capital (Lee, 1997; Devereux, Lockwood & Redoano, 2008; Marceau, Mongrain & Wilson, 2010);
- heterogeneity of firms in terms of their costs (Haufler & Stähler, 2009);
- compensation of tax revenues lost in effect of competition from other financing sources (Mendoza & Tesar, 2005).

The alternative string of taxation economics literature, begun by Tiebout (1956), states that tax competition can be positive as it leads to efficient spending on public goods and services. This efficiency comes from the fact that citizens in choosing optimal – from their perspective – relation between taxes paid and public goods obtained leave regions where the spending is inefficient to regions closer to their desired optimum. Administrative inefficiency can stem from over-taxation or under-taxation in the form of an imbalance with an amount of public goods supplied by a local government. It is important to note that the Tiebout hypothesis was embodied in the federalism postulate according to which local governments attract citizens by providing demanded relation between the tax-mix and public goods, with a role for a central government supplying public goods of country-wide character such as military. In the result, the 'voting with one's feet' process, caused by fiscal competition among tax jurisdictions, is considered to be positive as it increases social welfare measured as a sum of all people's utility functions.

A promising direction of development of the tax competition theory replaces perfect competition with a monopolistic competition (with a prominent role of transaction costs, including particularly transportation costs), assuming the existence of areas of fixed initial endowment of production factors, different in the centre and peripheries, and agglomeration effects resulting in an increase in capital productivity where it is concentrated (Baldwin & Krugman, 2004). This effect reduces the negative effects of harmful tax competition and forces a tax increase even above the equilibrium tax rate proposed by the traditional theory of tax competition. Taxes are raised in the centre and remain low in the periphery. This model may assume migration from remote areas to agglomerations if international trade is free (Ludema & Wooton, 2000), asymmetric tax competition (Haufler & Wooton, 1999), or autonomous convergence – where convergence of economies takes place – of tax rates on the periphery to those in the centre (Borck & Pflüger, 2006).

The recent theories of international tax competition are only partially reflected in the actual data. Tax burden is transferred from capital to labor which is a postulate of the traditional theory of asymmetric tax competition, and the tax effects of agglomeration are also observed (Kudła, 2013). Each group of models has therefore something to offer which calls for an integration of the two approaches.

1.3. Fiscal solvency

The theories of optimal taxation or tax competition between countries for production factors, or any of their expansions, do not fully correspond to the actual conditions of taxation when the problem of fiscal solvency arises. It is a well-known concept that during an economic crisis financing of government spending is more difficult due to an increase in debt servicing costs and difficulties or even inability to borrow. As emphasized by Mendoza and Tesar (2005), in such circumstances governments are more susceptible to an increase in debt servicing costs due to concerns about their fiscal solvency. Countries therefore may adjust taxation of capital, labor and consumption in order to ensure long-term solvency[3] and hamper harmful international capital tax competition. Despite a high degree of flexibility in the tax-mix, various types of taxes are, to different degrees, prone to such adjustments. For example, harmonization of consumption taxes in the European Union constrains their use as a source of financing government expenditure and forces adjustment in tax burden on labor and capital[4]. In practice,

3 Krogstrup (2002) phrases this with very accurate words: 'The wedge in the budget stemming from debt service must affect either the level of tax revenues or the level of primary expenditures, assuming that there is a limitation to deficit financing'. In fact, we observe a shift from revenue-based competition to spending competition, which is a key to understanding the functions of taxation. The tax-mix, incl. public borrowing, may be then viewed as the plane on which country functions change. This is in line with the reasoning of, for example, Sorensen (2006) and Bucovetsky (2005) who present a preference for public investment rather than public distribution as the former is more likely to attract foreign capital.

4 The harmonization of indirect taxes in the European Union has provided some security of national budgets to ensure money for providing public goods. However, in order to avoid the 'race-to-the-bottom' phenomenon the harmonization of direct taxes can be required, particularly those on capital. In 1990s there has been a lot of public debate on whether direct tax harmonization is possible and whether tax base harmonization is a better approach. The tax base harmonization requires countries to pass lax laws which provide for calculation of taxable profit or loss in the same way in all of them. Therefore, this necessitates all countries to have the same depreciation rules, deferred income rules, loss carry forward regulations, just to name a few.
This is not only politically but also practically difficult, as with such harmonization some countries win while others lose. Countries which are able to attract particularly

then, a significant reduction in capital taxes is not possible without an increase in labor taxes. The latter requires a low elasticity of labor income and is unpopular for social and political reasons. In effect, taxes on capital are lowered mainly in countries with relatively high taxes on capital income where an increase in labor income taxes is easier to force. Consumption taxes are, however, simpler to adjust, and to a lesser extent affect factors of production. They are also less apparent to taxpayers as they are included in prices of goods. Furthermore, their use may be motivated by the need to adjust for negative externalities (e.g. higher taxes on energy are justified by environmental protection, or higher taxes on cigarettes – by the concern of public health), violating one of the fundamental theorems of the optimal taxation literature, stating that taxes on final consumption goods should be uniform (Atkinson and Stiglitz, 1976). These advantages have neither capital taxes inducing capital outflow nor labor taxes distorting the labor market. Distortionary taxation (i.e. taxes on productive factors) has negative effect on economic growth (Shinohara[5], 2014), and as such should be minimized if a government pursues growth policy. Consumption taxes and taxes on immovable property should be used instead. Indeed, Krogstrup (2002) finds that if the tax competition-type analysis is extended to include public debt considerations, then debt service costs fall rather on labor and consumption than capital.

What then should an optimal tax structure look like in the light of the theoretical achievements made so far? The authors of *Tax by design* postulate the tax system to be 'designed to do least harm to the productive potential' of an economy, and 'viewed as fair' (p. 502), and they successively provide for a detailed list of normative guidelines for a 'good' tax system at play, which is much in line with what is briefly reviewed above.

---

capital by providing more favorable tax conditions for foreign direct investments, for example, via the use of special economic zones, lose this benefit through imposing the tax harmonization even if it takes only a form of harmonizing tax bases. However, the extent to which some countries lose while others win depends on the particular approaches taken. When the tax rate harmonization is considered, harmonizing at a higher tax rate will provide countries with more tax revenues, while simultaneously undermining their competitive position.
Besides analyzing the tax base and tax rate harmonization, the recent tax competition literature and public debate have focused on eliminating harmful tax competition – one that led to uneven playing field for all countries involved – such as location of enterprises in tax havens, non-market transfer prices or hiding of profits, among others. Again, these phenomena made a case for harmonizing tax systems.

5 Shinohara (2014) provides an extensive survey of theoretical and empirical studies of the relationship between a tax structure and economic growth.

2. The tendencies in European taxation

The total tax burden along with compulsory social contributions in the European Union can be considered as quite high in comparison to other developed areas. For example in 2012 taxes and social contributions totaled around 40% GDP-weighted average, higher than those in USA (around 25%), Japan (around 30%), Russia (35%) and Canada (below 30%) (Eurostat, 2014). The highest tax burden was recorded by western European Union members such as: Belgium, Denmark and France, while the lowest one for the eastern and central European countries. These included so-called new member states admitted to EU after 2003, such as Lithuania, Latvia and Bulgaria. However, it can be, to some degree, expected considering the EU's long-term focus on social welfare state which requires the provision of numerous public goods and services. The total tax burden measured as tax revenue-to-GDP ratio started to fall since 2000 but since the financial crisis this process has been hindered. Unfortunately the high level of tax burden can lower the international competitiveness of European countries.

It is noteworthy to point out that countries of EU differ greatly in institutional tax framework – this includes the centralized or federal establishment of tax regulation and the composition of tax policy mix. Fiscal autonomy of local governments on the tax field occurs only in four countries: Austria, Germany, Belgium and Spain. In general, we still have division into old members and the new one (admitted after 2003). The old member countries rely more heavily on direct taxation, whereas new member countries use to a greater extent the indirect taxation. At least partially this can be explained by the differences in the level of economic development and the effectiveness of tax administration. Richer countries have affluent societies allowing them to obtain more revenues from direct taxation, while poorer countries have to count more on revenues from indirect taxation such as VAT. Moreover, Scandinavian countries and United Kingdom obtain significant amount of revenues from direct taxation while social contributions are quite low. In contrast, Netherlands, France and Germany draw most of their revenues from social contributions financing social care systems. In the latter group of countries the revenues from direct taxes are relatively small.

The economic crisis had a significant impact on taxation patterns. Countries have faced a choice among various options of fiscal adjustment with two prevalent strategies. According to the first, some of the European countries decided to cut tax rates in order to relieve their taxpayers and hopefully spur economic growth. According to the Eurostat data, in the first place the taxes on labor have been lowered to induce people to take-up work and to relieve the overburdened social care system. The capital taxes were cut only moderately, possibly because governments did not believe that during recession the policy of low tax rates can attract substantial amount of new capital. Finally this led to decreasing EU's average tax rates and social contributions. Especially the lowest point of implied tax rates was recorded in 2010 and after that one can observe weak growth of implied tax rates.

According to the second strategy some countries decided to increase taxes. The most popular actions were to increase the Value Added Tax (VAT) as well as to introduce specific taxes such as bank taxes or surtaxes (Eurostat, 2014). Although tax revenues decreased in 2008 and 2009 in a result of the shrinking economy, the increase of tax burden undertaken by European Union members enlarged the tax revenues in 2011. In the next 2012, tax revenues calculated as a percentage of GDP went up in twenty-two EU countries, decreased in six, while remained stable in Cyprus (Eurostat, 2014).

However, it should be stressed that tax revenues expressed as a percentage of GDP provide an incomplete view because many countries experienced GDP downfall in the same time. For example, Greece noted the decline of tax revenues in 2012 but despite this the ratio of tax revenues to GDP has increased. This was evidenced because the drop of GDP was faster than the decline of tax revenues. The Greek economy has started with tax revenues decrease at the beginning of the crisis, reflecting mainly the lower economic activity. But already in 2011 the new taxes (such as tax on real estate) have been imposed to balance the deficit affected by the threat of debt insolvency (Eurostat, 2014).

3. The indebtedness problem

The difficulty in budget balancing with lower tax revenues encourages most of European governments to increase deficits and to engage in high debt financing. The data extracted from Eurostat shows that indebtedness in EU countries as a percentage of GDP has been steady rising since 2009 (see **Table 1**). This was particularly evident in southern European countries. The most worrisome of these was the very fast increase of the debt observed for: Ireland, Spain, Portugal and Greece. The highest increase peaking at over 32% in 2010 has been evidenced for Ireland. In the same year Spain and Portugal increased the net borrowings at over 11%. The one year before (2009) Greece noticed an indebtedness change of about 15%. Some part of these changes can be explained by the necessity of rescue for bank with toxic assets and some part would be a consequence of lower demand caused by the economic slowdown.

Table 1: *Net lending or net borrowing as a percentage of GDP for European Union countries*

GEO/TIME	2004	2005	2006	2007	2008	2009	2010	2011	2012	2013
Belgium	-0,2	-2,6	0,3	0,0	-1,1	-5,5	-4,0	-3,9	-4,1	-2,9
Bulgaria	1,8	1,0	1,8	1,1	1,6	-4,2	-3,2	-2,0	-0,5	-1,2
Czech Republic	-2,7	-3,1	-2,3	-0,7	-2,1	-5,5	-4,4	-2,9	-4,0	-1,3
Denmark	2,1	5,0	5,0	5,0	3,2	-2,8	-2,7	-2,1	-3,9	-0,7
Germany (until 199	-3,7	-3,3	-1,5	0,3	0,0	-3,0	-4,1	-0,9	0,1	0,1
Estonia	:	:	:	:	:	:	0,2	1,0	-0,3	-0,5
Ireland	1,4	1,6	2,8	0,2	-7,0	-13,9	-32,4	-12,6	-8,0	-5,7
Greece	:	:	-6,1	-6,7	-9,9	-15,2	-11,1	-10,1	-8,6	-12,2
Spain	0,0	1,2	2,2	2,0	-4,4	-11,0	-9,4	-9,4	-10,3	-6,8
France	-3,5	-3,2	-2,3	-2,5	-3,2	-7,2	-6,8	-5,1	-4,9	-4,1
Croatia	-5,1	-3,7	-3,3	-2,5	-2,7	-5,9	-6,0	-7,7	-5,6	-5,2
Italy	-3,6	-4,2	-3,6	-1,5	-2,7	-5,3	-4,2	-3,5	-3,0	-2,8
Cyprus	-3,8	-2,2	-1,1	3,2	0,9	-5,6	-4,8	-5,8	-5,8	-4,9
Latvia	-1,0	-0,4	-0,6	-0,6	-4,0	-8,9	-8,2	-3,4	-0,8	-0,9
Lithuania	-1,5	-0,5	-0,4	-1,0	-3,3	-9,3	-6,9	-9,0	-3,2	-2,6
Luxembourg	-1,0	0,2	1,4	4,2	3,3	-0,5	-0,6	0,3	0,1	0,6
Hungary	-6,4	-7,9	-9,4	-5,1	-3,7	-4,6	-4,5	-5,5	-2,3	-2,4
Malta	-4,4	-2,7	-2,6	-2,3	-4,2	-3,3	-3,3	-2,6	-3,7	-2,7
Netherlands	-1,8	-0,3	0,2	0,2	0,2	-5,5	-5,0	-4,3	-4,0	-2,3
Austria	-4,8	-2,5	-2,5	-1,3	-1,5	-5,3	-4,5	-2,6	-2,3	-1,5
Poland	:	:	:	:	:	:	-7,6	-4,9	-3,7	-4,0
Portugal	-6,2	-6,2	-4,3	-3,0	-3,8	-9,8	-11,2	-7,4	-5,5	-4,9
Romania	-1,2	-1,2	-2,2	-2,9	-5,6	-8,9	-6,6	-5,5	-3,0	-2,2
Slovenia	-2,2	-1,5	-1,3	-0,1	-1,8	-6,1	-5,7	-6,2	-3,7	-14,6
Slovakia	-2,3	-2,9	-3,6	-1,9	-2,4	-7,9	-7,5	-4,1	-4,2	-2,6
Finland	2,2	2,6	3,9	5,1	4,2	-2,5	-2,6	-1,0	-2,1	-2,4
Sweden	0,3	1,8	2,2	3,3	2,0	-0,7	0,0	-0,1	-0,9	-1,3
United Kingdom	-3,6	-3,5	-2,9	-3,0	-5,1	-10,8	-9,6	-7,6	-8,3	-5,8

Source: Eurostat database (2014).

While high debt levels have been commonly experienced by countries around the globe, this crisis was different as it affected the European Union members. On one hand, EU membership should help to obtain additional financing from countries with high credibility like for example Germany. On the other hand, functioning in a pan-European context did not allow for undertaking various financial actions to resolve the mounting crisis, such as currency devaluation or common bond issue. Therefore, the institutional obstacles prevent the corrective actions taken by national governments to resolve the crisis.

The problem with debt was coupled with high current account imbalance over roughly the same period 2008-2011. For example the relation of Greece's and Portugal's import/export to GDP approached -10%. In particular, import of southern European countries exceeded their export which indirectly indicated structural economic weakness. This indicated the lack of competitive power, intensified by imprudent fiscal policy. A popular belief was that some countries enjoyed a high standard of living even though their economies could not support it.

The consequence of such policy has been an economic real adjustment (occurring without currency devaluation, because the latter was impossible) mainly by the high increase of unemployment.

Since monetary aggregates could not adjust properly, the countries experiencing the outburst of debt and low productivity were forced to implement austerity fiscal policy cutting expenses and increasing taxation. The economy was stalled, as unemployment drastically rose. People did not have enough money to maintain prior standard of living which led to social turmoil and unrest. In such a context the institutions of European Union agreed to lend money, firstly to Greece and later to other countries, in order to restore real economic fundamentals of economies to help them repay current debt servicing and to built new competitive positions. However, the recovery is slow and the EU has been criticized not only for providing the ineffective financial help but also for the disadvantages of currency union which have been pinpointed intensively.

We would like to analyze the situation of the indebtedness taking into account all European countries regardless their participation in European Union. This is important for the future econometric analysis but also for the embedment of fiscal policy in the context going beyond the institutional problems of EU or Eurozone itself. Therefore one can observe the net debt changes of 34 European countries were fluctuating over the period 2002-2011. As presented on **Figure 1**, the average value of the net debt change in 2002 was about 2,5%, then it fell to about 0,5% in 2007 and dramatically rose to 5,5% in 2009, as a consequence of financial crisis. Range of standard deviation (in grey) gives the outlook of average differences between countries. Positive values of relative net debt ratios are understood as a surplus and negative as a deficit.

Obviously there were countries with permanently good position, located above the confidence interval. Norway was the only country which was above grey area over full investigated period. Before crisis (up to 2007), these were also: Belgium (2006), Bulgaria (2004, 2006, 2007), Denmark and Finland (2002, 2005, 2006, 2007), Estonia (2002, 2003, 2005, 2007), Iceland (2005, 2006, 2007), Ireland (2005, 2006), Lichtenstein (2007), Luxembourg (2002, 2007), Spain and Sweden (2004, 2005, 2007). In 2008, debt above 0 was kept by: Bulgaria, Cyprus, Denmark, Finland, Luxembourg, Netherlands and Sweden and in later years it happened for: Estonia, Hungary and Sweden.

There were also countries with permanently high change of new debt, located below grey line. Before crisis these were: Cyprus and Malta (2002), Czech Republic (2002), Croatia (2002), Turkey (2002, 2003), Hungary (2002, 2004, 2005, 2006, 2007), Poland and Portugal (2004), France (2003), Greece (2004, 2005, 2007). In

2008, these were Greece, Ireland and Latvia, and in recent years: Greece (2009, 2010, 2011), Spain (2009), Ireland (2009, 2010, 2011), Portugal (2009) and United Kingdom (2009, 2010).

Figure 1: *Net debt of countries in 2002-2011*

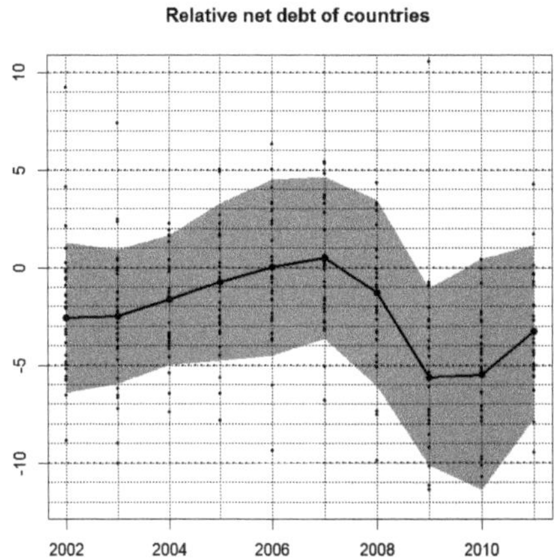

Source: Own analysis on data from IMF

The debt changes occurs not only in time but also in space. This particularly interesting in the context of econometric evaluation of spacial sopillover relations which can be affected by tax competition or followers effects. The basic comparisons on relative net debt changes in space and time are presented on **Figure 2**. The situation in 2002 was better (lower debt) and more balanced than in 2011. Unfortunately in 2011, not all the countries managed to improve their debt performance. Moreover, in the last year of observation (2011) several spatial clusters can be distinguish. They consist of: western countries (Spain, France, UK, Ireland), central countries (Belgium, Netherlands, Denmark, Germany, Switzerland, Italy, Austria, Czech Republic) and northern countries (Norway, Sweden, Finland). This pattern is absolutely different than the one observed in 2002, when most countries provided very similar debt policy. This uniformity was probably determined by the formation of monetary union and the introduction of euro in 1999, when the compliance with fiscal rules was much greater and it was decisive for the participation of given countries in the Eurozone project.

Figure 2: *Spatial distribution of relative net debt changes in 2002 and 2011*

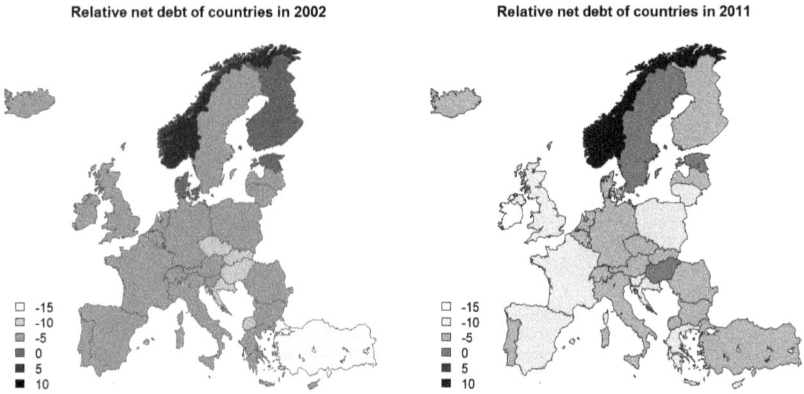

Source: Own analysis on data from IMF

Nevertheless, to get a deeper insight into details of spatial relations, we need to provide the spatial analysis with so called Moran's I spatial autocorrelation statistic. This statistic measures processes and patterns that appear throughout the territory. It depends on the difference between the test based on the covariance matrix and the average value. The observations are weighted with special distance matrix. The value of Moran's I statistic staying between $-1 < I < 0$ indicates negative correlation so the similar values match less often than random. The values between $0 < I < 1$ mean positive correlation so similar values match more often than random. In graphical presentation, the relation between debt changes is expressed by the spatial Moran Scatterplot. These are two dimensional (x,y) dot charts, where x is a given variable and y is its spatial lag – the average of variable values in neighboring locations. With standardized values, one can easily assess how far from the average the given region and its neighbors are. The location in (x,y) quarters can be mapped to see the spatial patterns (scatterplot map).

Figure 3 presents Moran scatterplot with inverse squared distance matrix (the weights of observations in the matrix are the inverses of squared distance between countries) in two separate years: 2002 and 2011. This type of matrix was chosen because the econometric analysis performed in Chapter 5 confirms that this type of weighting reflects very well spatial interdependences. **Figure 4** presents mapping of Moran scatterplot's points according to quarters of (x,y) coordinate system. When both x and y are positive ($x>0$, $y>0$) then quarter is called HH (high-high). This means that the value of the variable is high and the same is for the neighbors. These analytics allow for interpretation of cluster differences as well as on cluster dynamics in debt performance. Obviously Fig. 3 and Fig. 4 should be analyzed together.

As on Fig. 4a and Fig. 5a, in 2002, Bulgaria, Slovenia, Austria and Spain were located in II quarter (HL), which means that their debt ratio was high and their neighbors kept the debt ratio lower. In 2002, the best debt ratios in countries and their neighborhood were on the north (clusters of Iceland, Ireland, UK, Scandinavian countries, Belgium, Netherlands, Switzerland, Baltic countries). After the crisis, in 2011, cluster of Scandinavian countries and Baltic countries did not change. There were two visible spatial trends: weakening of western countries cluster and strengthening of eastern countries cluster. It can be summarized that positions of central countries stayed similar, and positions of eastern and western countries were exchanged. This could be probably caused by the greater involvement of western countries in financial crisis and by the higher impact of banks problems on the government performance and the size of debt. Spatial concentration of debt is also clearly visible over time.

Figure 3: *Moran scatterplot of relative net debt in a) 2002 and b) 2011*

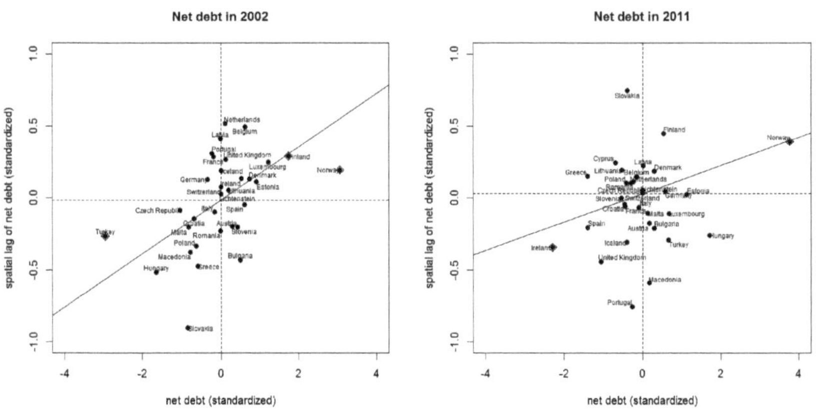

Source: Own analysis on data from IMF

Figure 4: *Spatial distribution of relative net debt in a) 2002 and b) 2011*

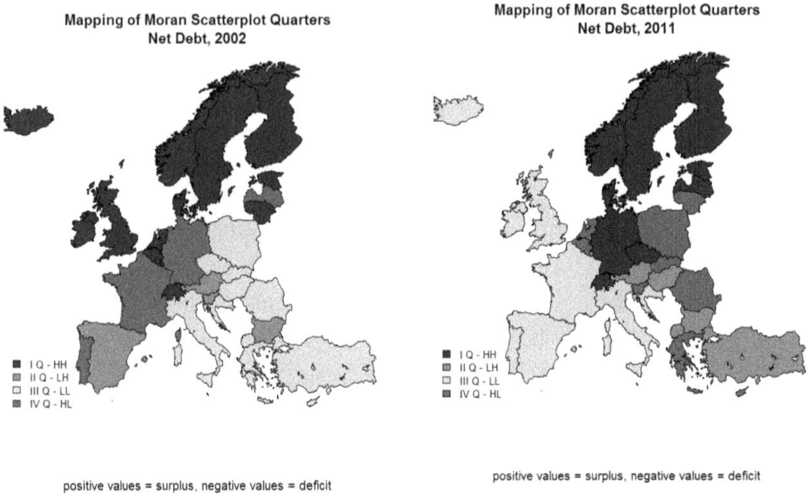

Source: Own analysis on data from IMF

4. The tax adjustment

The economic crisis entwined with debt crisis made a significant impact on taxation issues and influenced the debate over competitiveness of taxation systems in the European Union. Increasing indebtedness and simultaneously declining economic conditions have led to an increase in tax burden. For example in Greece, taxes on labor increased from 30%[6] of total taxes and labor contributions in 2008 to 37% in 2012. In the same time the total general government revenue to GDP increased only slightly from 41% in 2008 to 45% in 2012. In the case of Spain, taxes on labor increased from 51.6% to 53% as a total in 2012 but the greatest increase was experienced from 2007 to 2008, while government revenue as a percentage of GDP remained approximately the same 37.5% (Table 2 provides full data for implicit tax rate on labor from Eurostat, 2014).

The increase of tax burden was necessary to finance increasing debt payments generated by earlier borrowings. It is noteworthy that countries with debt

6 The tax rates in this chapter refer to the implied tax rates. It means the relation of tax revenues of given type of tax to the size of tax base. The value of implied tax rates is provided by Eurostat (2014).

problems in the first place increased taxes on labor. The labor taxation was preferred because labor is perceived as one of the less mobile production's factors and it cannot avoid higher taxation easily.

Table 2: *Ratio of taxes and social security contributions on labor income to total compensation of employees*

geo\time	2005	2006	2007	2008	2009	2010	2011	2012
Belgium	43,6	42,4	42,4	42,4	42	42,7	42,9	42,8
Bulgaria	33,2	29,7	30,4	27,4	25,7	23,5	24,2	24,5
Czech Republic	41,3	41,1	41,7	39,9	37,6	38,4	39	38,8
Denmark	37,1	36,9	36,6	36,6	34,8	34,2	34,3	34,4
Germany	37,5	38,1	38,2	38,6	38	37,2	37,3	37,8
Estonia	33,8	33,6	33,9	33,8	34,9	36,6	35,7	35
Ireland	25,4	25,3	25,5	24,5	25,1	25,9	28,2	28,7
Greece	33,3	32,3	33,3	32,9	30	31,5	30,9	38
Spain	32,4	32,9	33,7	32,4	31,4	32,6	32,9	33,5
France	39,3	39,3	39	39	38,6	38,1	38,8	39,5
Croatia	29,6	30,3	30,8	31	31,3	31,1	29,7	29,2
Italy	41,2	40,9	42,4	43	42,6	42,6	42,3	42,8
Cyprus	24,4	23,9	23,9	24,6	26,2	26,9	26,8	28,8
Latvia	33,2	33,1	31,1	28,4	29,2	33,1	33,3	33
Lithuania	34,9	33,6	33,1	32,7	32,6	31,5	31,5	31,9
Luxembourg	29,9	30,3	31	31,6	31,6	31,8	32,5	32,9
Hungary	38,4	38,9	41	42,3	40,2	38,4	38,2	39,8
Malta	22,5	22,7	21,2	21,2	21,7	21,6	22,5	23,3
Netherlands	32,3	35,1	35,6	36,8	35,9	37	37,5	38,5
Austria	40,8	40,9	41	41,3	40,3	40,5	40,8	41,5
Poland	33,8	35,4	34	31,7	30,9	30,3	32	33,9
Portugal	22,4	23,1	23,7	23,5	23,6	24,2	25,4	25,4
Romania	28,1	30,1	30,2	27,3	28,6	30	33	30,4
Slovenia	37,6	37,3	35,9	35,9	35,1	35	35,3	35,6
Slovakia	32,9	30,5	31,1	32,7	31,4	32,2	31,6	32,3
Finland	41,6	41,6	41,3	41,2	40,1	39	39,5	40,1
Sweden	43,6	42,9	41,2	41,2	39,4	39,1	38,9	38,6
United Kingdom	25,9	25,9	26,1	26,2	24,7	25,6	25,8	25,2

Source: Own calculation on Eurostat data (Eurostat, 2014).

On the same background as for debt, the analysis of implied tax rates levels and their changes can be conducted. In general the tax policy in Europe consisted of: the declining taxation of labor, increasing and then decreasing taxation of capital and increasing taxation of consumption. However the significance of particular taxes in total tax revenues of a country is different, as it depends on tax rate and the volume of tax base. Following EUROSTAT Taxation Trends (2014), the share of consumption taxation in total tax burden in EU was about 29%, the share of labor taxation about 51% and the share of capital taxation reached 20%. Historically, the lowest level of this tax-to-GDP ratio was noted in 2010. Cutting taxes in most cases involved the tax rates reduction. The average changes of implied tax rates on consumption, labor and capital are presented on **Figure 5**.

Figure 5: *Implied tax rates in Europe 2002-2011*

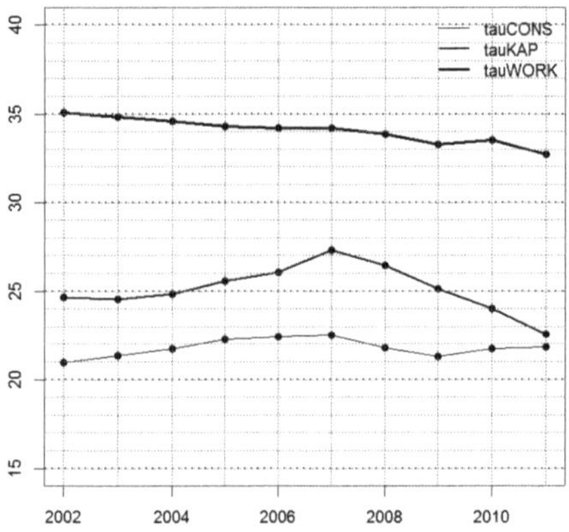

Source: Own analysis using data from EUROSTAT

However, those aggregates do not present the individual tax rates and time shifts in fiscal policy. Therefore the detailed analysis of three separate types of tax burden is subsequently provided to capture the general tendencies in tax policy mix.

4.1. Implied tax rate on capital

The first analyzed tax rate is the implied tax rate on capital. This kind of tax is paid mainly as a tax on corporate income and as a tax on stock of capital and wealth. The general trend over last decade was the increase of this tax rate in 2007. It was probably intended to lessen the speculation which was expected to boost financial crises (**Figure 6**). However, during next year, implied tax rates on capital were declining on average. The average implied tax rate on capital was close to 25±2% in the investigated period, although there were countries with tax rates much below or above this level. Capital tax rates higher than 30% were observed in almost all analyzed years in: Belgium, Denmark, France, Italy, Norway, Portugal and United Kingdom. Capital tax rates lower than 15% were observed in Baltic states: Estonia, Latvia, and Lithuania.

Figure 6: *Implied tax rate on capital in 2002-2011 in Europe.*

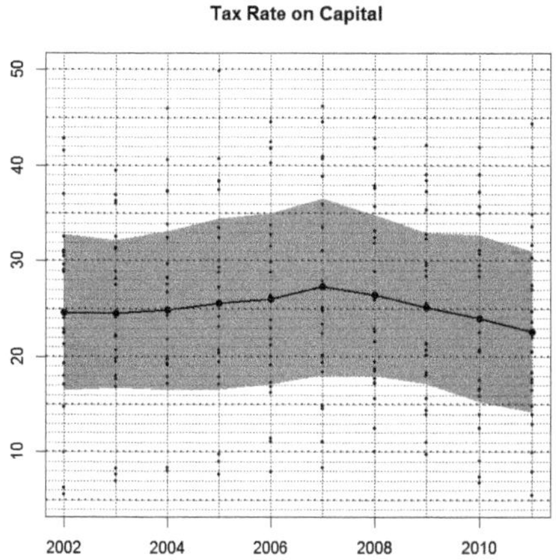

Source: Own analysis on data from EUROSTAT

Fluctuations from year to year (in time dimension) do not change the general spatial pattern. However, these annual fluctuations could be stronger and weaker. The weakest fluctuations were observed in: Norway, Finland and Belgium but the highest (almost 10 times higher) in: Cyprus, Spain, Netherlands, Denmark, Estonia, Latvia and Lithuania. Spain and Portugal started in 2002 with almost the same tax rate (31,1% and 32,6%), but in 2011 the difference was significant. Portugal tax rates on capital were oscillating around 32% (with peak of 37,6% in 2008). Spain went up to 44,5% in 2007 and then dramatically went down to 22,5% in 2011. The same pattern happened in Denmark (from 30,8% in 2002 through 46,2% in 2007 to 22,5% in 2011), in Cyprus (from 24% in 2002 through 41% in 2007 to 24,7% in 2011) and in Latvia (from 9,9% in 2002 through 17,3% in 2008 to 9,9% in 2011).

Spatial distribution of tax rates on capital (**Figure** 7) proves that those rates in most cases stay fixed among countries. These patterns evidence only few separate capital tax policies: a) to keep tax rates stable and high (Norway, UK, France, Portugal, Italy) or b) to find the optimal level of taxation by trial and error (with high variability) on: low level of tax rates (Latvia, Lithuania, Estonia); intermediate level (Netherlands, Greece, Ireland, Slovakia) or high level of tax rates (Cyprus, Spain, Denmark) or c) to choose the strategy of average tax rates (about 20%-30%) with low variability. The last strategy is chosen by the most countries from the sample.

Figure 7: *Implied tax rates on capital in: a) 2002; b) 2011*

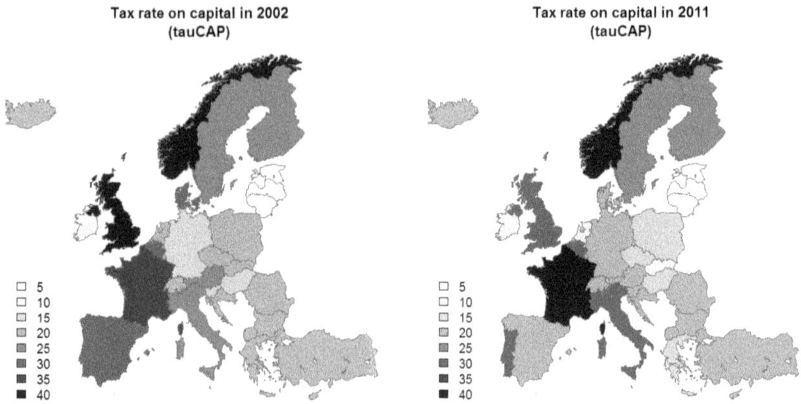

Source: Own analysis on data from EUROSTAT

Spatial statistics (**Figure 8, Figure 9**) confirm relatively constant geographical distribution of implied tax rates on capital. Regarding the changes of outliers, Netherlands (LH) and France (HH) moved further from the average level to – lower tax in Netherlands and to – higher tax in France.

Figure 8: *Moran scatterplot of implied tax rate on capital in a) 2002 and b) 2011*

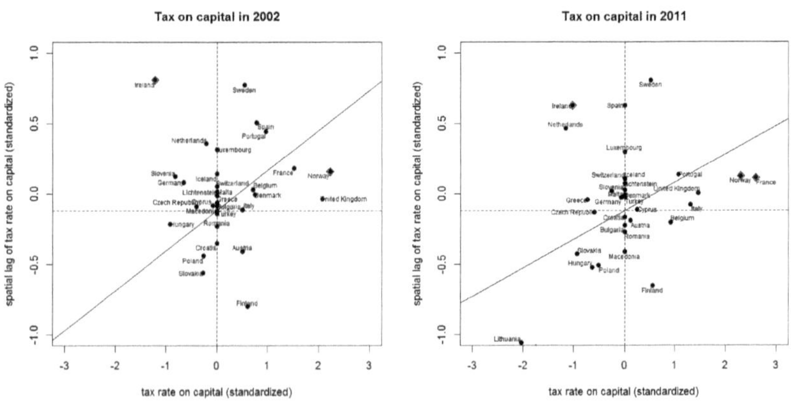

Source: Own analysis on data from EUROSTAT

Figure 9: *Spatial distribution of implied tax rate on capital in a) 2002 and b) 2011*

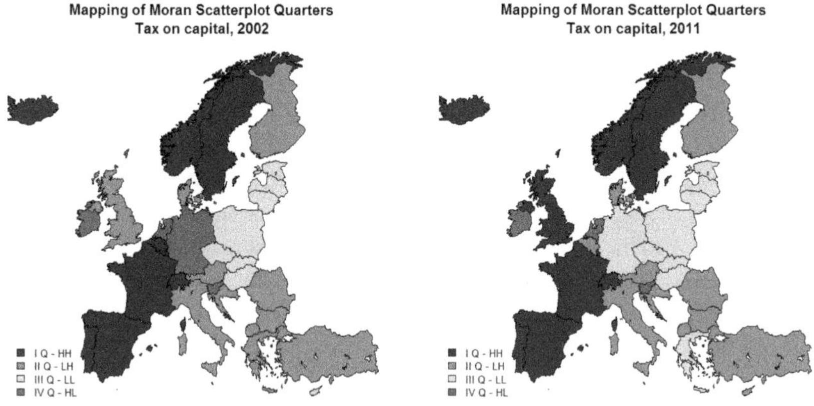

Source: Own analysis on data from EUROSTAT

The fluctuations magnitude of implied tax rate on capital allows for putting a hypothesis that at least in some countries it is set in an experimental way (**Figure 10**). The highest fluctuations in this tax rates were observed in: Cyprus, Spain, Netherlands, Denmark, Estonia, Latvia and Lithuania. Especially one could observe extreme changes of tax level in years 1995-2014 for the main component of capital taxation – the tax rate on corporate income (CIT).

Figure 10: *Highest fluctuations of implied tax rates on corporate income*

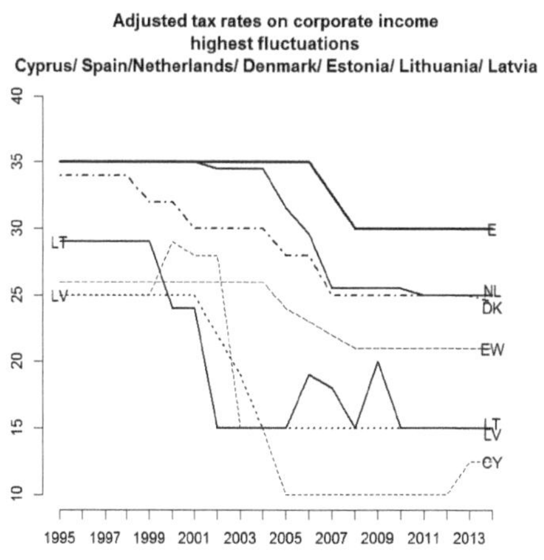

Source: Own analysis on data from EUROSTAT Taxation Trends 2014

4.2. Implied tax rate on labor

The second tax rate is an implied labor tax rate. This rate is very important for the all economies. Its main components are: personal income tax, social contributions and payroll taxes. As one can observe from the aggregate plot (**Figure 11**), the general trend between European countries was to lower this tax. On average, it dropped from 35% to 32.5% in period 2002-2011. However, disparities between countries are significant and even double between extreme values. The implied tax rate above 40%, which is frequently over the grey corridor of standard deviation, was in: Austria, Belgium, Czech Republic (till crisis), Finland, France, Italy and Sweden (till crisis). Below 25% implied tax rate, which is usually below grey corridor of standard deviation (with exception of the last year) was: Cyprus, Malta and Portugal.

Figure 11: *Implied tax rate on labor in 2002-2011 in Europe.*

Source: Own analysis on data from EUROSTAT

As one can notice on **Figure 12** the spatial structure of labor tax has changed significantly over the last 10 years. The number of countries with tax rate higher than 40% decreased from 8 countries (Austria, Belgium, Czech Republic, Finland, France, Hungary, Sweden) to 3 countries (Austria, Belgium, Italy). Significant reductions were especially evident in: Scandinavian countries, France and Czech Republic.

Figure 12: *Implied tax rates on labor in: a) 2002; b) 2011*

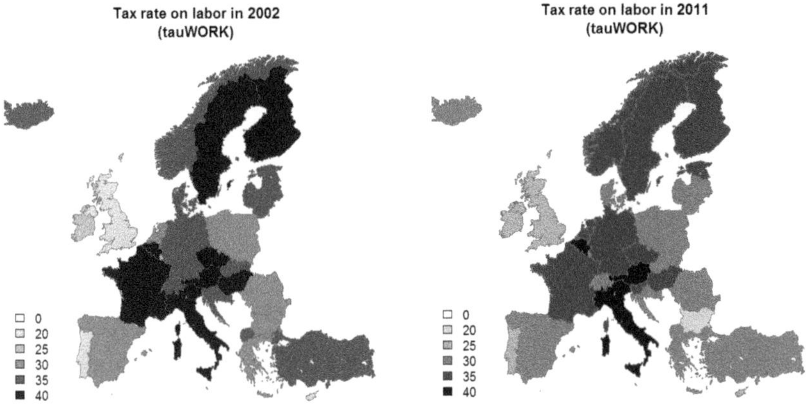

Source: Own analysis on data from EUROSTAT

At least four geographical clusters with similar level of tax burden can be distinguished in the case of implied tax on labor. The changes of implied tax rates on labor in clusters are presented on **Figure 13.** The pattern revealed in the analysis only slightly resembles the one obtained for the implied tax rates on consumption. Relatively unchanged remains northern cluster because only Ireland does not fit the pattern. However, the organization of central and southern Europe regarding the implied tax rate on labor is different. One should extract group of islands and coastal countries (Portugal/ Cyprus/ Malta/ Ireland/ UK), which impose much lower tax rates on labor than the rest of countries. Eastern countries have, on average, lower tax rates than western countries. Even when in general tax rates were declining, some countries were raising the labor tax burden. There is evident convergence of tax rates on labor in time, especially for northern and eastern countries.

Figure 13: *Implied tax rates on labor in geographical clusters*

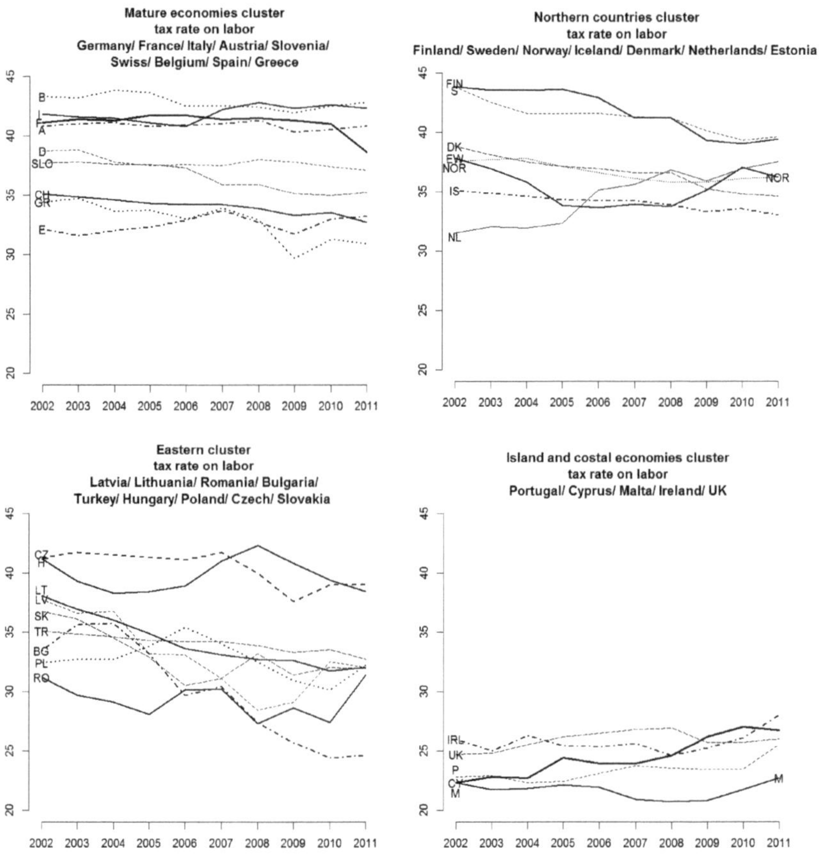

Source: Own analysis on data from EUROSTAT

Spatial analysis with the use of spatial weights matrix (**Figure 14**) confirms results obtained for clusters. Very clear is the convergence of low-tax (LL) countries to the average. These are UK, Portugal and Ireland. In the case of Belgium (HL) tax burden remained the same but the values of tax rates in neighborhood increased significantly which affected to a large degree the position of this country. The spatial clusters are directly apparent on the **Figure 15**.

Figure 14: *Moran scatterplot of implied tax rate on labor in a) 2002 and b) 2011*

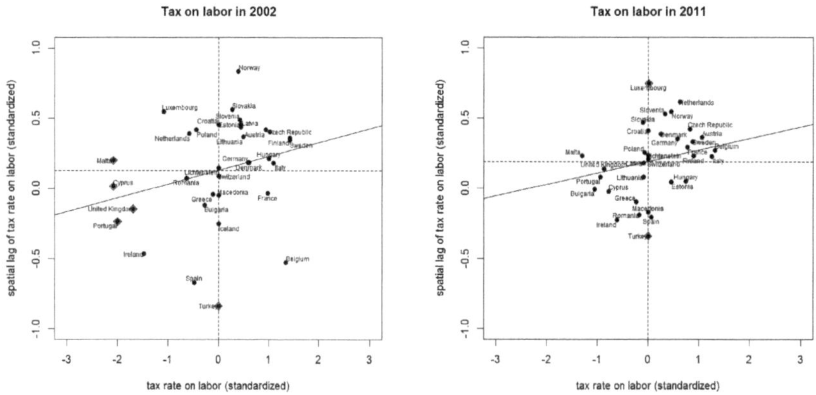

Source: Own analysis on data from EUROSTAT

Figure 15: *Spatial distribution of implied tax rate on labor in a) 2002 and b) 2011*

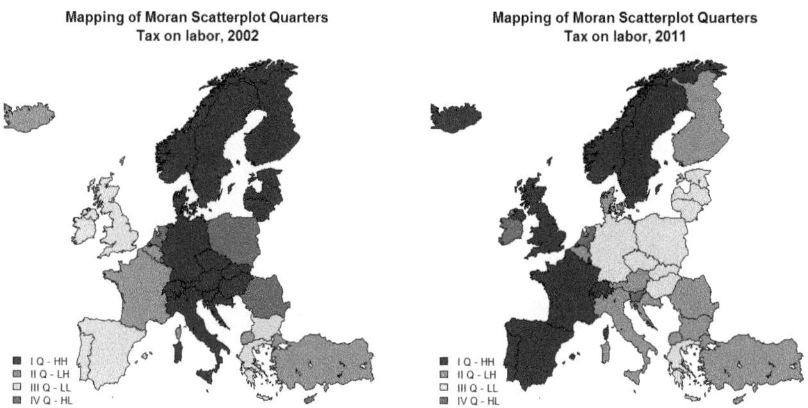

Source: Own analysis on data from EUROSTAT

4.3. Implied tax rate on consumption

The third tax rate is an implied consumption tax rate. Tax rate on consumption mainly encompasses value added taxes (from 56% of consumption taxation in Italy to 74% in Sweden) but also excise taxes on energy (with mineral oil taxes), tobacco and alcohol (Eurostat, 2014). Tax rates on consumption are well diversified across Europe. On average the implied consumption tax rates oscillate around 22-23%. However, the interval calculated on standard deviation $(\bar{x} - sd(x), \bar{x} + sd(x))$ does not cover all rates applied in 34 analyzed countries (**Figure 16**). Below grey corridor (16,5%-18.3%) always were: Greece, Italy, Lithuania and Spain, and before the crisis additionally Romania with UK and after the crisis: Latvia, Portugal and Slovakia. Above grey corridor (25%-27%) there are always: Denmark, Finland, Hungary, Luxembourg, Norway and Sweden and before the crisis there were also: Ireland and Netherlands, and after the crisis: Estonia and Netherlands.

The slight drop in consumption tax rates which appeared in 2008 and 2009 can be explained as not the VAT decline (as such a decline was absent in most countries) but the consequences of financial crisis: curbing consumption of primary goods, usually taxed with lower tax rates, and involuntary inventory build-ups, which were the basis for VAT refunds (Eurostat, 2010). Value added tax rates were constantly increasing since 2009. The level of average VAT rate in 28 EU countries was stable from 2000 till 2008 and circulates around 19,5%±0.1. However in period 2008-2014 the average level of taxation rose from 19,5% to 21,5% (Eurostat, 2014).

Figure 16: *Implied tax rate on consumption in 2002-2011 in Europe*

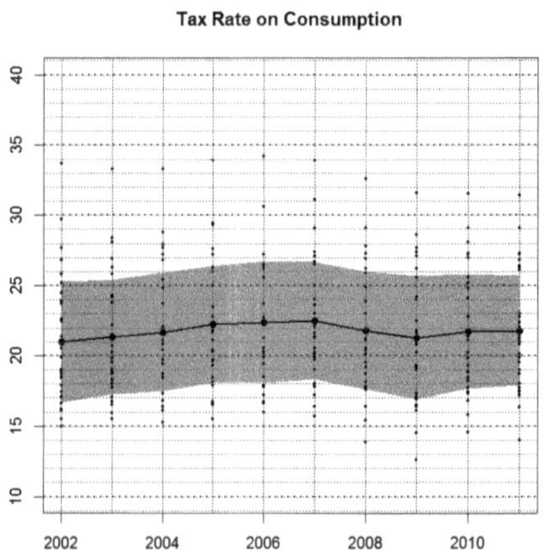

Source: Own analysis on data from EUROSTAT

On the maps for both years 2002 and 2011 (**Figure 17**) the spatial clusters of similar tax rates are clearly visible. Precisely we can distinguish three spatial clusters: northern countries, western countries and Germany-linked countries. We can also track tax rate changes in those groups (**Figure 18**). In the discussed period all clusters run relatively stable policy of consumption taxation.

Northern countries: Finland, Sweden, Norway, Iceland, Ireland, Denmark, Netherlands and Estonia keep their taxes permanently high (at level close to 27%). One can see also tax policy changes: Estonia follows tax rates strategy of northern neighbors, especially Finland. Two islands countries, Ireland and Iceland are following the same pattern of taxation of consumption. However in recent years, these two countries depart distinctly from Northern countries cluster. However, their tax rates still remain too high (about 23%) to be a part of western cluster (about 18%) or Germany-linked cluster (about 21%).

Germany-linked countries are neighbors of Germany and include: Poland, Czech Republic, Austria, Switzerland and Belgium. Slovakia is the country escaping this cluster, because it sets the lowest tax rates on consumption in the region. This is most likely undertaken to improve the competitiveness. Last and relatively small group of countries formulate east-south cluster with Turkey, Romania and Bulgaria.

Observing the geopolitical distribution of implied tax rate on consumption, it seems that countries try to avoid tax competition on consumption taxes. Strategy of similar tax rates helps to avoid intensive cross-border speculative flows of goods and services. There are few exceptions from this rule: Slovakia, with competitively low tax rates in the region, and oppositely Hungary with very high tax rates – much higher than the neighbors. We can guess that strategy of Slovakia is to attract foreign purchases and the strategy of Hungary is to cover the high debt (from -8.8% in 2002 to -4.45% in 2010) under assumption that people prefer stability over the mobility for lower taxes.

Looking at tax changes from the perspective of economic power, one can see that northern countries cluster follow their own patterns and do not intend to follow the rest of Europe. Their economic links are so strong, that Estonia, which is pretending to find its own position in the international environment, decided to imitate their tax rates policy probably to better integrate with Finland, which is its closest significant neighbor. Second cluster, central-continental gets the rhythm of changes from Germany. Poland, Czech Republic, Austria, Switzerland and Belgium follow the policy of tax consumption after their biggest partner country. It is interesting that France seems to behave contrary to Germany in the consumption tax rate changes but together with other countries from western cluster.

Figure 17: *Map of implied tax rates on consumption*

Source: Own analysis on data from EUROSTAT

Figure 18: *Geographical clusters in consumption taxation*

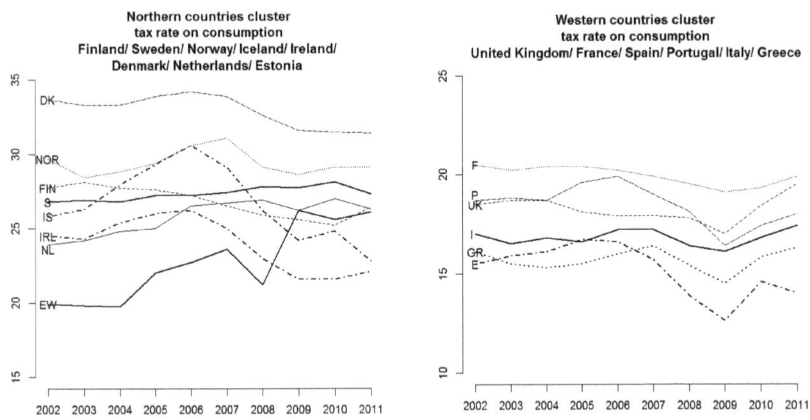

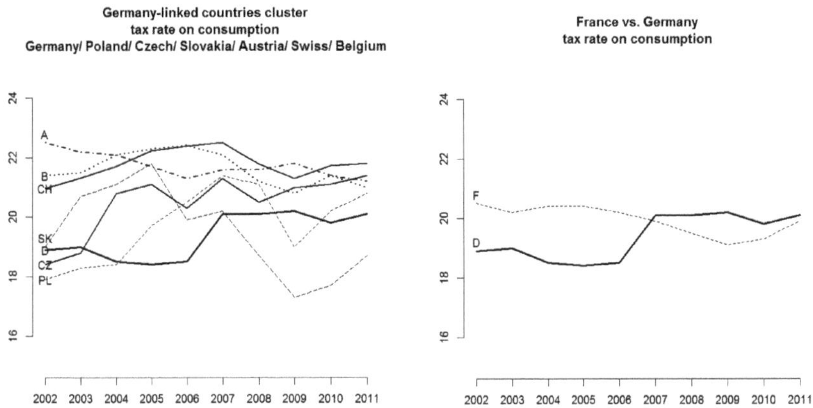

Source: Own analysis on data from EUROSTAT

From Moran Scatterplot (**Figure 19**) one can easily see that in 2011 there were only few outliers like Estonia and Hungary (second quarter, HL, x>0, y<0) with high tax rates, surrounded by countries with low tax rates. Second group of countries is low consumption tax countries – Portugal, Lithuania and Spain (fourth quarter, LL, x<0, y<0). The third visible group of countries are northern countries (Sweden, Norway, Denmark, Netherlands, Finland) and Luxembourg kept in the first quarter (HH, x>0, y>0). The rest of countries stabilize their taxes close to each other. Moreover this pattern is constant over time. For example in 2002, the quarter HH was almost the same but with Iceland and Slovenia. This means that even after 10 years, relative position of northern countries remains similar: they tax consumption with higher rates than 1 standard deviation from the European mean. In 2002 Estonia was in the 3rd not 2nd quarter. This shift, mainly caused by the increase of x and the slight decrease of y, means that Estonia has increased their tax and their neighbors did not change their policy a lot. The clusters are apparent on the **Figure 20**.

Figure 19: *Moran scatterplot of implied tax rate on consumption in a) 2002 and b) 2011*

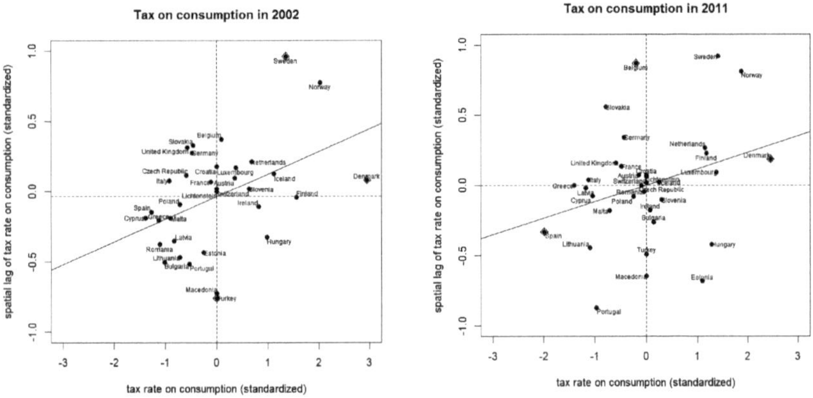

Source: Own analysis on data from EUROSTAT

Figure 20: *Spatial distribution of implied tax rate on consumption in a) 2002 and b) 2011*

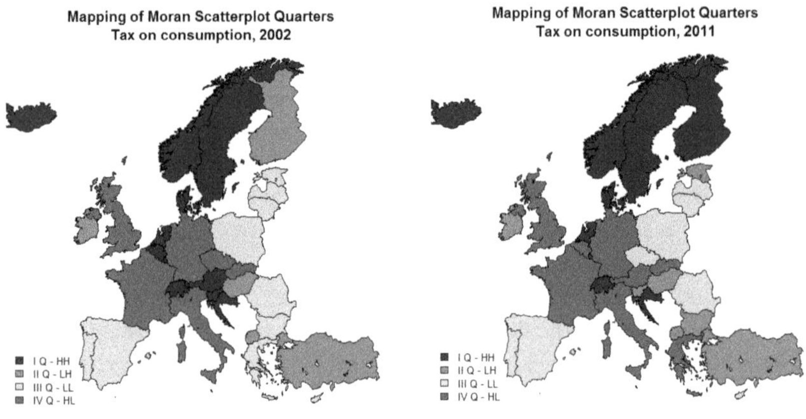

Source: Own analysis on data from EUROSTAT

4.4. Changes of tax policy mix

In the analysis of fiscal policy mix it is worth to assess what kind of tax changes were performed in the last 10 years in Europe. A table below (**Table 3**) presents the distribution of possible compositions of tax changes. We have distinguished nine scenarios: eight scenarios with possible non-zero changes and one scenario, where at least one tax rate stayed unchanged. Changes were calculated on the annual basis from implied tax rates. Pattern '++-' means that implied tax rates on consumption and capital were increased and the implied tax rate on labor was decreased.

Table 3: *The distribution of changes in tax rates: consumption/capital/labor*

Pattern	+++	++-	+--	---	+-+	-++	-+-	--+	*with 0*
Freq	12%	17%	13%	14%	10%	4%	10%	9%	10%

Source: Own analysis on data from EUROSTAT

Tax rate on consumption was increased in 52% situations and decreased in 37% situations. Tax rate on capital was increased in 43% and lowered in 46% situations. Tax rate on labor was increased in 35% situations and decreased in 54% situations. This confirms asymmetries in fiscal policy. In general, trend was to lower labor tax rate and to increase consumption tax rate with taxation of capital without clear tendency.

The most often change was to increase tax rates on consumption and capital and to lower tax rate on labor (17%). The least popular strategy was to decrease tax rate on consumption together with the increase of taxes on capital and labor (4%). In 10% situations, one of the tax rates stayed unchanged.

Not only direction, but also the magnitude of changes can be tracked. Table 4 presents the distribution of tax rates changes over the analyzed period 2002-2011.

Table 4: *The distribution of the amount of tax rates changes*

delta (p.p.)	*deltacons*	*deltacap*	*deltawork*	*Total tax rate change*
(-∞, -10)	0%	1%	0%	1%
(-10, -1)	8%	**32%**	17%	34%
(-1, -0,5)	14%	9%	12%	6%
(-0.5, 0)	22%	11%	**31%**	12%
(0, 0.5)	**32%**	14%	23%	10%
(0.5, 1)	12%	9%	8%	8%
(1, 10)	12%	24%	8%	30%

Source: Own analysis on data from EUROSTAT

All three tax rates have their modes (dominant values) at different level of tax rate change. For tax on consumption the most often were changes between from 0 p.p. to 0.5 p.p., in case of tax on capital these were between -10 p.p. to -1 p.p., and in case of tax on labor between -0.5 p.p. and 0 p.p.

One can also construct an index measuring the total magnitude of tax changes (see **Table 4**). It is simply the total sum of tax rates changes. This kind of indicator can help to detect the general direction of tax rates changes. The dominant types of tax rate changes in the sample were either negative and relatively big (more than 1 p.p.) (34% of total number of observations) or positive and relatively big (more than 1 p.p.) (30% of total number of observations).

Positive changes of all tax rates (increase in all implied tax rates) were observed mainly in 2007 (12 countries decided to rise all tax rates). Negative changes of all tax rates (decrease in tax rates) took place in 2008 (12 countries) and especially in 2009 (17 countries). The most popular strategy (++-) was practiced mainly in the period 2004-2006.

Chapter 2
The static tax competition models with debt

1. Introduction

On the one side the economics of taxation concentrates on tax competition models with two tax instruments and without the impact of debt. On the other side most of models capturing the impact of debt apply general equilibrium approach. Together these two approaches do not allow for the modeling of the tax changes triggered by the solely interaction of debt and tax rates with respect of predictions implied by tax competition model. However, it is worth of interest to check whether the predictions of model of tax competition with many tax rates and the debt are consistent with results obtained in the up-to-date literature. Precisely we would like to concern the equilibrium solutions of three tax rates and bonds issue. Trying to fulfill the existing gap in the theory, the two static tax competition models are developed with: three tax instruments, debt and cross-border ownership of capital and bonds. Our proposition is one-period only and does not include savings. The first model is the one-country model with indirect impact of tax competition on capital and consumption, where a government controls three tax rates and debt is set as exogenous. The maximization concerns the utility of representative consumer of the country. The model helps to derive some relatively simple implicit function on tax rates on capital and consumption showing the possible determinants of taxation in the multi-tax world.

The second proposition involves two-country static model with two endogenous tax rates (on capital and labor), bonds issuance controlled by government and one tax rate (on consumption) treated as a constant parameter. It means that taxation of consumption is assumed to be exogenous but the issuance of bonds is not. In comparison with the former model this change of the optimization objective greatly simplifying the final solution and making it unique. Subsequently this allows for the calculation of two-tax Nash equilibrium for both countries. Notwithstanding, the analytical equilibrium solution is troublesome because it consists of many expressions and parameters. Therefore the derivation of the result provides less clear-cut analytical formulas than traditional results known from tax competition models of one or two tax instruments. To deal with this problem a numerical investigation of different scenarios is provided, involving: the impact of debt servicing cost changes and some possible harmonized policies, like for example taxation of financial transaction or imposition of common income tax base. The special attention is put on the role played by the debt (bond issuance), according to the so called fiscal solvency hypothesis. This hypothesis states that with many tax instruments the countries remain solvent and they only adjust the composition of tax rates without inducing "race to the bottom" of capital taxation. The impact of debt changes is calculated only for the debt servicing costs because the bonds issuance simply works in the opposite way. This means that when debt servicing costs increase then it induces the same tax changes as the decrease of bonds issuance or decline of its price on the primary market (when bonds are sold for the first time). The impact of debt on tax rates seems to be crucial in explaining the changes of tax rates during insolvency crisis but unfortunately up-to-date is not well captured by the existing economic theory.

2. The one-country static model of taxation

The purpose of the government is to set three tax rates (on capital income – τ_k, labor income – τ_l and consumption – τ_c) to maximize the utility of a representative consumer[7]. All consumers are the same and derive utility from consumption of private good (c) and of the consumption of public good (g). The utility of a representative consumer (U) is an increasing function of the both consumption goods size. The objective function which is maximized takes the usual form:

$$\max_{\tau_k, \tau_l, \tau_c} U(c, g) \tag{1}$$

The consumer in this model lives only for one period, so she has no reason to save and the whole consumer's income is spent on consumption. The consumption consists of domestic consumption taxed in home country and foreign consumption of goods. Domestic consumption is financed by three sources of income: income of capital after taxes, income of labor after taxes and net repayment of debt. Foreign consumption can be financed from domestic sources of income or from foreign income of comsumers.

Capital employed in production in the country (k) is compensated at a level equal to its marginal productivity f_k (the last is the derivative of production function f with respect of capital). Part α of capital is owned by the consumer, and the rest ($1 - \alpha$) – by non-residents. Only part s of capital income is taxed in the country,

---

7 The basic model in this chapter is presented in enhanced form and described in (Kudła et al., 2014*).

and the rest (1–s) – is shifted abroad avoiding domestic taxation. The consumer disposable income derived from capital invested at home is equal to $(1-\tau_k)s\alpha f_k k$.

The consumer is also the country's only labor force. The labor is immobile and its supply is assumed to be constant ($\bar{l}$). Labor is remunerated according to f_l the marginal product (the derivative of production function f with respect of l). Net income from labor is therefore $(1-\tau_l)f_l\bar{l}$. The production function is sensitive to the changes of capital invested and the capital has positive impact on the productivity of labor $f_{lk} > 0$.

The consumer receives also income from the repayment of government debt ε_t, net purchases of bonds b_t, sold at a discount γ. Moreover, consumption is financed from income earned abroad z[8]. The income earned abroad is sensitive to the taxation at home but the functional form of this relation is unknown. Therefore we expect that the only observable effect on z exerts taxation of consumption. Summing up all sources of income the formula for total domestic consumption takes the following form:

$$c = (1-\tau_c)[(1-\tau_k)s\alpha f_k k + (1-\tau_l)f_l\bar{l} + \varepsilon_t - \gamma b_t] + z \tag{2}$$

This formula unavoidably determinates taxes paid to the government budget from:

- capital income not transferred abroad – $\tau_k s f_k k$,
- labor income – $\tau_l f_l \bar{l}$,
- domestic consumption – $\tau_c[(1-\tau_k)s\alpha f_k k + (1-\tau_l)f_l\bar{l} + \varepsilon_t - \gamma b_t]$.

---

8 This form of consumption function and parameter z should be explained in greater detail because it seems unintuitive. Let's suppose that the share n of the consumer's total income – a sum of the domestic (y_d) and the foreign (y_{fn}) income – is spent in the country. Real private consumption is hence given by (τ_c and τ_c^* are, respectively, domestic and foreign consumption tax rates):

$$c=(1-\tau_c)n(y_d+y_{fn})+(1-\tau_c^*)(1-n)(y_d+y_{fn}),$$

$$c=[(1-\tau_c)n+(1-\tau_c^*)(1-n)]y_d+[(1-\tau_c)n+(1-\tau_c^*)(1-n)]y_{fn},$$

$$c=[(1-\tau_c)+(1-\tau_c^*)\frac{1-n}{n}]y_d+[(1-\tau_c)+(1-\tau_c^*)\frac{1-n}{n}]y_{fn},$$

$$c=(1-\tau_c)y_d+(1-\tau_c^*)\frac{1-n}{n}y_d+[(1-\tau_c)+(1-\tau_c^*)\frac{1-n}{n}]y_{fn},$$

which can be expressed as:

$$c=(1-\tau_c)y_d+z$$

where $z=(1-\tau_c^*)\frac{1-n}{n}y_d+[(1-\tau_c)+(1-\tau_c^*)\frac{1-n}{n}]y_{fn}$. Each of the two parts of the formula contains unknown variables (τ_c^*, n or y_{fn}) which we treat as beyond the control of home country government. Eventually we obtain the equation (2):

$$c=(1-\tau_c)y_d+z=(1-\tau_c)[(1-\tau_k)s\alpha f_k k+(1-\tau_w)f_l\bar{l}+\varepsilon_t-\gamma b_t]+z.$$

In addition, the government receives tax revenues from consumption tax (τ_c) of purchases (z^*) made by foreigners ($\tau_c z^*$)[9], and those from the sale of bonds (γb_t). It is assumed that foreign purchases in home country z^* depend on k, τ_c and τ_k. The demand for home country goods is stimulated by exogenous factors affecting foreign income and all factors increasing the income obtained by foreigner from home country. The latter involves the capital income (explicit – taxed in home country and implicit – avoiding home taxation), the net income from bonds, and the effects on productivity triggered by the level of capital invested in home country.

Government revenues finance public goods (g) and debt service (repayment) (ε_t):

$$g + \varepsilon_t = \tau_k s f_k k + \tau_l f_l \bar{l} + \tau_c[(1-\tau_k)s\alpha f_k k + (1-\tau_l) f_l \bar{l} + \varepsilon_t - \gamma b_t] + \tau_c z^* + \gamma b_t$$

which can be expressed after simplification as:

$$g = \tau_k s f_k k + \tau_l f_l \bar{l} + \tau_c[(1-\tau_k)s\alpha f_k k + (1-\tau_l) f_l \bar{l} + z^*] + (1-\tau_c)(\gamma b_t - \varepsilon_t) \quad (3)$$

There are two constraints imposed on fiscal policy. Firstly, the taxation of consumption cannot be too high ($\tau_c \leq \tau_{c\max} \rightarrow \tau_{c\max} - \tau_c \geq 0$). This can be justified by: political reasons (inability to raise taxes harming the poor), the negative impact of consumption taxes on redistribution or economic growth, high welfare losses (dead-weight loss/excess burden of taxation) or legal restrictions (such as the upper limit of the VAT rate in the European Union). If the consumption tax could be arbitrarily high, then the government would consider this tax as a kind of lump-sum tax, providing no distortion to production factors. Therefore the high taxation of consumption would be the remedy for the inability of other taxes increase and it should allow for the financing public good and debt servicing costs.

Secondly, there should be a maximum interest rate that the government is able to pay for debt servicing ($r_\varepsilon \leq r_{\varepsilon\max} \rightarrow r_{\varepsilon\max} - r_\varepsilon \geq 0$). Above this threshold value all borrowing by the government would be discontinued ($b_t = 0$), and the budget must be balanced. This strictly addresses the fiscal solvency concept with maximum available payment causing the bankruptcy of a country. The maximum level of debt interest rate depends on the level of taxation of capital, labor and consumption and the size of the original debt (ε_t). The relation of interest rate on debt and tax revenues should be negative but the relation with tax rates is ambiguous because higher tax rates can hint higher financial needs of the country's

9 Consumption is assumed to be taxed on the origin principle. Although it is the destination principle that is generally applied (e.g. in European Union), the origin principle is practiced in border trade and retail electronic commerce.

government or problem with repayment. In ordinary situation higher tax rates should provide higher revenues if government operates on the increasing part of the Laffer curve. This should stimulate the decrease of interest required on financial market for the bonds.

The possibility of borrowing by the government sheds new light on its choice of the tax-mix policy. Purchases of bonds– unlike taxes – are voluntary which means that the sign of $\varepsilon_t - \gamma b_t$ is not predetermined. It seems the consumer would prefer this difference to be positive but then he/she runs the risk of higher taxation of capital, labor or consumption that is not neutral. However, If the consumer would accept negative value of $\varepsilon_t - \gamma b_t$, then it would be possible to lower tax rates and consequently to reduce the distortion caused by taxation in the economy. In the considered case this difference is assumed positive and activates higher taxation. The latter supposition better fits to the crisis time and problems with fiscal solvency.

The optimization problem can be written as a Lagrange function:

$$L(\tau_k, \tau_l, \tau_c) = U(c, g) + \lambda(\tau_{c\max} - \tau_c) + \mu(r_{\varepsilon\max} - r_\varepsilon) \tag{4}$$

The necessary (Kuhn-Tucker) conditions can be presented in five subsequent points:

1.

$$L_{\tau_k} = U_c\, c_{\tau_k} + U_g\, g_{\tau_k} + \mu(r_{\varepsilon\max} - r_\varepsilon)_{\tau_k} = 0$$

$$L_{\tau_k} = U_c\,(1-\tau_c)\left\{s\alpha k(1-\tau_k - f_k) - \frac{\partial(\gamma b_t)}{\partial \tau_k} + (1-\tau_l)\bar{l}\frac{f_{lk}}{f_{kk}}\right\} +$$

$$U_g\left\{\begin{matrix}(\tau_l + (1-\tau_l)\tau_c)\bar{l}\dfrac{f_{lk}}{f_{kk}} + sk[\tau_k + f_k + \alpha\tau_c(1-\tau_k - f_k)] - \tau_c\dfrac{\partial(\gamma b_t)}{\partial \tau_k} + \dfrac{\partial(\gamma b_t)}{\partial \tau_k} + \\ [\tau_k + \tau_c(1-\tau_k)]s\alpha\dfrac{f_k}{f_{kk}} + \tau_c\left[\dfrac{\partial z^*}{\partial \tau_k} + \dfrac{\partial z^*}{\partial k}(1-\alpha)\dfrac{1}{f_{kk}}\right]\end{matrix}\right\} - \mu\frac{\partial r_\varepsilon}{\partial \tau_k} = 0$$

2.

$$L_{\tau_l} = U_c\, c_{\tau_l} + U_g\, g_{\tau_l} + \mu(r_{\varepsilon\max} - r_\varepsilon)_{\tau_l} = 0$$

$$L_{\tau_l} = U_c\,(1-\tau_c)\left\{-\frac{\partial(\gamma b_t)}{\partial \tau_l} - f_l\bar{l}\right\} + U_g\left\{(1-\tau_c)\left[\frac{\partial(\gamma b_t)}{\partial \tau_l} + f_l\bar{l}\right]\right\} - \mu\frac{\partial r_\varepsilon}{\partial \tau_l} = 0$$

3.

$$L_{\tau_c} = U_c\, c_{\tau_c} + U_g\, g_{\tau_c} + \lambda(\tau_{c\max} - \tau_c)_{\tau_c} + \mu(r_{\varepsilon\max} - r_\varepsilon)_{\tau_c} = 0$$

$$L_{\tau_c} = U_c\left\{-\left[(1-\tau_k)f_k s\alpha k + \varepsilon_t - \gamma b_t + (1-\tau_l)f_l\bar{l}\right] - (1-\tau_c)\frac{\partial(\gamma b_t)}{\partial\tau_c} + \frac{dz}{d\tau_c}\right\} +$$

$$U_g\left\{(1-\tau_k)f_k s\alpha k + \varepsilon_t - \gamma b_t + (1-\tau_l)f_l\bar{l} + z^* + \tau_c\left[\frac{\partial z^*}{\partial\tau_c} - \frac{\partial(\gamma b_t)}{\partial\tau_c}\right] - \frac{\partial(\gamma b_t)}{\partial\tau_c}\right\} - \lambda - \mu\frac{\partial r_\varepsilon}{\partial\tau_c} = 0$$

4.

$$L_\lambda = (\tau_{c\max} - \tau_c) \geq 0 \text{ and } \lambda \geq 0 \text{ and } (\tau_{c\max} - \tau_c)\lambda = 0$$

5.

$$L_\mu = (r_{\varepsilon\max} - r_\varepsilon) \geq 0 \text{ and } \mu \geq 0 \text{ and } (r_{\varepsilon\max} - r_\varepsilon)\mu = 0$$

The listed conditions describe the derivatives of Lagrange function with respect of three tax rates and two parameters (λ and μ). The two latter are used to capture the impact of constraints.

3. The optimal taxation in the one-country model

Here only the simplest case is considered when both constraints of the optimization problems are not binding[10]. This means precisely that consumption tax rate can be set arbitrary and the cost of debt is not exceeding the maximal acceptable level (algebraically it is equivalent of $\mu = 0$ and $\lambda = 0$). In such a case, the marginal rates of substitution between public good and private should satisfy the subsequent three equations:

$$\frac{U_g}{U_c} = -\frac{(1-\tau_c)\left\{s\alpha k(1-\tau_k - f_k) - \gamma\frac{\partial r_\varepsilon}{\partial\tau_k}\left[\frac{db_t}{dr_\varepsilon} - b_t\right] + (1-\tau_l)\bar{l}\frac{f_{lk}}{f_{kk}} + (1-\tau_k)\frac{f_k}{f_{kk}}\alpha s\right\}}{(\tau_l + (1-\tau_l)\tau_c)\bar{l}\frac{f_{lk}}{f_{kk}} + sk\left[\tau_k + f_k + \alpha\tau_c(1-\tau_k - f_k)\right] + (1-\tau_c)\gamma\frac{\partial r_\varepsilon}{\partial\tau_k}\left[\frac{db_t}{dr_\varepsilon} - b_t\right] + \left[\tau_k + \alpha\tau_c(1-\tau_k)\right]s\frac{f_k}{f_{kk}} + \tau_c\left[\frac{\partial z^*}{\partial\tau_k} + \frac{\partial z^*}{\partial k}(1-\alpha)\frac{1}{f_{kk}}\right]} \quad (5a)$$

(from derivative L_{τ_k})

10 The cases with binding constraints are described in (Kudła *et al.*, 2014) but in general the constrained solutions are simpler version of the unconstrained case.

$$\frac{U_g}{U_c}=\frac{(1-\tau_c)\left\{\frac{\partial(\gamma b_t)}{\partial\tau_l}+f_l\bar{l}\right\}}{f_l\bar{l}-\tau_c\left[\frac{\partial(\gamma b_t)}{\partial\tau_l}+f_l\bar{l}\right]+\frac{\partial(\gamma b_t)}{\partial\tau_l}}=1 \tag{5b}$$

(from derivative L_{τ_l}) and

$$\frac{U_g}{U_c}=\frac{(1-\tau_k)f_k s\alpha k+\varepsilon_t-\gamma b_t+(1-\tau_l)f_l\bar{l}+(1-\tau_c)\gamma\frac{\partial r_\varepsilon}{\partial\tau_c}\left[\frac{db_t}{dr_\varepsilon}-b_t\right]-\frac{dz}{d\tau_c}}{(1-\tau_k)f_k s\alpha k+\varepsilon_t-\gamma b_t+(1-\tau_l)f_l\bar{l}+z^*+\tau_c\frac{\partial z^*}{\partial\tau_c}+(1-\tau_c)\gamma\frac{\partial r_\varepsilon}{\partial\tau_c}\left[\frac{db_t}{dr_\varepsilon}-b_t\right]} \tag{5c}$$

(from derivative L_{τ_c}).

The marginal rates of substitution have to be the same for each relation of derivatives. This (from 5b) implies the MRS equals to 1 in each case. Therefore the model predicts optimal provision of public goods and lack of "race to the bottom" effect on capital taxation. It should be emphasized that labor tax τ_1 can be set arbitrarily and the level of debt has no impact on the tax rates (the formulas with debt cancel each other in all equations, if we require the MRS to be 1 according to 5b). The result is consistent. If a country is always credible then the debt level is irrelevant for the cost of debt, and taxation and debt are set independently.

The formula on τ_k can be calculated from (5a), as:

$$\tau_k=-\frac{f_{lk}\bar{l}}{(1-\alpha)s(f_k+kf_{kk})}-\frac{kf_k f_{kk}}{f_k+kf_{kk}}-\frac{\tau_c[(1-\alpha)\frac{\partial z^*}{\partial k}+f_{kk}\frac{\partial z^*}{\partial\tau_k}]}{(1-\alpha)s(f_k+kf_{kk})}-\frac{\alpha}{1-\alpha} \tag{6}$$

Unfortunately, the derived equation for capital tax cannot be interpreted directly because the relation is implicit[11] and depends on the functional form of: production, cross-country functions of foreign consumption and the dependence of *k* on tax rates. Therefore, we can only say that the taxation of capital is determined by four factors. The first refers to the interaction with labor; the second to the remuneration of capital; the third modifies the value of trans-border consumption and the last is responsible for the tax export effect.

Simultaneously from (5c) we receive another important formula: $\frac{-\frac{\partial z}{\partial\tau_c}}{z^*+\tau_c\frac{\partial z^*}{\partial\tau_c}}=1$, which implies the value of consumption tax:

11 The calculation for the example of production function is included in (Kudła *et al.*, 2014), together with detailed discussion of properties of the results.

$$\tau_c = -\frac{z^* + \frac{\partial z}{\partial \tau_c}}{\frac{\partial z^*}{\partial \tau_c}} \quad (7)$$

According to obtained the result, taxation of consumption should depend on the sensitivity of taxation of domestic and foreign purchases and on the total volume of foreign purchases in the country. As before without clear identification of functions z and z^* the detailed prediction of the consumption tax is not available. However it should be stressed that this formula does not involve the taxation of labor and capital inside. This may indicate that total adjustment of tax rates is incurred by other taxes.

Summing up the results one can see that countries should remain solvent if they have at least three tax instruments. This means that they can offer the public goods effectively and support the existing level of debt without going bankrupt. In this case there is no impact of debt on tax rates because the taxation of labor can be increased to cover the enlarged financial needs of government. Only capital income taxation is set with respect of other types of adjustment in the economy (on labor, capital, consumption and the share of domestic property in capital). Contrary to this, consumption tax is determined by the sensitivity of trans-border purchases and labor tax is not directly affected. This suggests that if a government has to cover the higher payment of debt then the basic tax adjustment should involve labor taxation. However, the model does not take into account the impact of this tax on unemployment or more generally on labor supply. The adjustment of capital taxation is less obvious because it has been driven by conflicting forces.

4. Basic assumptions of Nash equilibrium model

The one-country model does not allow for the simulation of fiscal policies because reaction of foreign countries is assumed constant. To deal with this problem the two-country model with Nash equilibrium tax rates can be applied. Unfortunately the one-country model cannot be transformed to the version with two interacting countries. This is because solutions of the system of equations involve nonlinear relations implying several roots. Especially the problem arises when we calculate consumption tax rate which depends on two other tax rates. This greatly complicates the fiscal policy analysis because solutions with tax rates in the range zero-one are unstable and vary with the value of parameters. This ambiguity can be omitted by slight change of the government's objective. Instead of three taxes, the objective can involve two taxes and bond issuance optimization. Now the maximization involves the citizens' consumption with constraint imposed on the tax revenues fulfilling the budgetary needs. These needs are linked with the level of public goods and the repayment of debt. In comparison with one-country model we assume that higher level of private consumption leads inevitably to higher utility and higher welfare. The proposed maximization produces a result which leads to a Nash equilibrium which is unique. Despite the uniqueness of the final equilibrium the analytical formula for this result is too long and too complex to be presented here. Therefore the conclusions about properties of the solution are derived using numerical example curbing the tax rates size to the span zero-one. The numerical result strives to capture the impact of debt parameters on the equilibrium state and similarly the effects induced by some other interesting variables.

The model starts with two symmetrical countries competing for capital in non-cooperative game. The total sum of available capital in both countries is set constant and equals to K. The capital invested in home country is denoted k and in foreign country k^*. The capital investment in the country reacts to the capital taxation $k(\tau_k)$ and $k^*(\tau_k^*)$. This reaction is direct and refers to the home/foreign capital tax rates. At the same time the capital investment is also affected by the second country taxation in indirect way. This impact is determined by the interdependence with constant capital endowment because we can describe the invested capital as a function of home or foreign capital taxation: $K-k^*(\tau_k^*)=\mathrm{k}$ – in home country or $K-k(\tau_k)=k^*$ – in foreign country. Therefore the capital investment in any country is determined jointly by both tax rates on capital income. Capital can be invested at home or abroad, so a part of the capital α is owned by the residents, and the rest, $1-\alpha$, comes from the foreign country. The α is set exogenously at the beginning of the period. It entails the tax-export effect (Eijffinger & Wagner, 2002) and modifies the capital tax competition. The respective value for the foreign country is α^*, and represents the share of foreign capital owned by local residents. According to this, the home residents share in capital located in foreign country is $1-\alpha^*$. The parameters α and β refer further to shares of direct investment and portfolio investment (only in bonds) in the home country and parameters with asterisks to similar shares in foreign country[12].

In each country there are three tax rates on[13]: capital income, τ_k /(τ_k^*), labor income, τ_l /(τ_l^*), and consumption, τ_c /(τ_c^*), and three debt instruments: debt servicing cost, ε /(ε^*), issuance of bonds, b /(b^*) and the discount factor, $\gamma<1$ /($\gamma^*<1$).

12 To simplify the consideration parameter of tax shifting s is omitted. However, any model with s can be calculated as well as the same model without this parameter (or $s=1$). In general, models with s lower than 1 predict higher taxation of capital. This is because s is constant, so every time the part of capital income is "not shifting" abroad and can be taxed higher to compensate the loss of budget revenues.

13 Asterisks in all cases denote the foreign country's values.

The bonds can be purchased by residents and non-residents. There is no tax on the income generated by bonds (this is true in the basic version of the model but this assumption will be repealed later when the transaction tax would be imposed). The share of bonds held by residents in the home country is β, and the nonresidents posses the rest of the debt $1-\beta$. The same applies to the foreign country and the respective figures are marked as β^* and $1-\beta^*$. Both kinds of shares are exogenous but later we will simulate their impact on the equilibrium tax rates, because they are crucial to the explanation of different types of tax rates adjustment. For simplicity there is no savings in the model.

In the equilibrium tax rates on capital income do not exert pressure on the capital invested in both countries. This is consistent with the most tax competition models when tax rates are set optimally. Sometimes this refers to the conclusion that tax competition does not exist in the equilibrium. However the fear of capital outflow abroad drives the capital tax rates behavior. The changing fiscal parameters in the one or both countries disturb the equilibrium and this triggers the tax rates adjustment to the new stability. The described process allows for considering one period model only because we search for the tax parameters stabilizing the choice made by taxpayer/consumers and sustaining the equilibrium. It seems plausible to assume that short term value of capital and labor are relatively stable and the capital can be moved between countries but labor cannot. Therefore labor supply is assumed to be constant, $\bar{l}$, $\bar{l}^*$and immobile. For simplicity there is no unemployment. The production function is the same in both countries, concave and twice differentiable. Capital and labor are remunerated according to their marginal products, f_k, $f^*_{k^*}$ *and* f_l, $f^*_{l^*}$, respectively. The second derivatives of production function are negative and the mixed derivatives are positive (labor and capital positively affect each other productivity)

Consumer budget constraint

The home country net income y, consists of five components: 1) the α share of net income of capital invested at home, $(1-\tau_k)\alpha f_k k$, 2) the $(1-\alpha^*)$ share of net income of capital invested abroad, $(1-\tau_k^*)(1-\alpha^*)f^*_{k^*}k^*$, 3) net income of domestic labor, $(1-\tau_l)f_l\bar{l}$, 4) the β share of net income of home bonds, $\beta(\varepsilon-\gamma b)$, and 5) the $(1-\beta^*)$ share of net income of foreign bonds, $(1-\beta^*)(\varepsilon^*-\gamma^* b^*)$:

$$y = (1-\tau_k)\alpha f_k k + (1-\tau_k^*)(1-\alpha^*)f^*_{k^*}k^* + (1-\tau_1)f_l\bar{l} + \beta(\varepsilon-\gamma b) + (1-\beta^*)(\varepsilon^*-\gamma^* b^*) \quad (1a)$$

The respective foreign country income is constructed similarly:

$$y^* = (1-\tau_k^*)\alpha^* f^*_{k^*}k^* + (1-\tau_k)(1-\alpha)f_k k + (1-\tau_l^*)f^*_{l^*}\overline{l^*} + \beta^*(\varepsilon^*-\gamma^* b^*) + (1-\beta)(\varepsilon-\gamma b). \quad (1b)$$

Since the model is one period only, net income (1a) is fully consumed ($y=c$). However it can be spent at home or abroad, with the share of domestic spending equal to δ. Since consumption expenditure is taxed, the total consumption of residents is given by:

$$\begin{aligned} c &= (1-\tau_c)\delta y + (1-\tau_c^*)(1-\delta)y, \\ c &= [1-\delta\tau_c - (1-\delta)\tau_c^*]y. \end{aligned} \tag{2a}$$

Similarly, the total consumption of foreigners is given by:

$$\begin{aligned} c^* &= (1-\tau_c^*)\delta^* y^* + (1-\tau_c)(1-\delta^*)y^*, \\ c^* &= [1-\delta^*\tau_c^* - (1-\delta^*)\tau_c]y^*. \end{aligned} \tag{2b}$$

Consumption in both countries consist of income spent at home and abroad after local taxation. The parameter of home purchases is constant and exogenous. This means that taxes do not change the preferences for foreign goods and services. This could be true in the short term.

Current account balance

The capital income and payments of debt flow between countries. Therefore the value of these payments should be balanced providing the condition for current account equivalence. The current account is balanced in both countries if and only if:

$$(1-\delta)y-(1-\delta^*)y^* = (1-\beta^*)(\varepsilon^*-\gamma^*b^*)+(1-\tau_k^*)\alpha^* f_{k^*}^* k^* - (1-\beta)(\varepsilon-\gamma b)-(1-\tau_k)\alpha f_k k, \tag{3}$$

where the left-hand side of (3) represents the foreign trade balance, and the right-hand side – net payments generated by non-residents investment in both countries. The first part of right side presents cashflow from foreign debt for home country residents. The second element is the income of foreign direct investment received by home country residents. The two other parts mirror the same kinds of income but for foreign residents. In this model there are no unknown sources of income financing foreign purchases like in the one-country model.

Government budget constraint

The home government receives: $\tau_k f_k k$ from taxation of capital income, $\tau_l f_l \bar{l}$ from taxation of labor income, $\tau_c \delta y$ from taxation of domestic consumption of residents, $\tau_c(1-\delta^*)y^*$ from taxation of domestic consumption of non-residents, and $\gamma b - \varepsilon$ from bonds issuance over the repayment of debt. Purchases of bonds are – unlike taxes – voluntary, so the sign of net borrowings is not pre-determined. However, government strives to keep this value as non-negative in the short-term, because it helps to decrease distortionary taxes on capital and labor. This assumption implies that positive revenues of capital and labor taxes are necessary to finance the part of debt servicing. The rate of consumption tax is, to some degree, determined by international regulations, such as the upper limit of the VAT rate in the European Union, and to some degree, by the possibility of cross-border trade in commodities (the higher the rate, the more goods may be traded to avoid the higher tax burden at home). Therefore, we assume that it is set exogenously (as a value parameter) in the model, and it cannot be raised unilaterally (by discretion of one of the governments). It should be also stressed that consumption tax is not affected by the production function, opposite to capital and labor taxes, and can be viewed as less harmful than taxes imposed on production factors.

Formally home government maximizes consumption of the residents, choosing τ_k, τ_l, and b, with respect to:

$$\bar{g} = \tau_k f_k k + \tau_l f_l \bar{l} + \tau_c c + \gamma b - \varepsilon, \tag{4a}$$

where $\bar{g}$ denotes government expenditure which is fixed. The similar maximization problem can be set for the foreign government:

$$\max_{\tau_k^*, \tau_l^*, b^*} c^*$$

with respect to:

$$\bar{g}^* = \tau_k^* f_{k^*} k^* + \tau_l^* f_{l^*} \bar{l}^* + \tau_c^* c^* + \gamma^* b^* - \varepsilon^*. \tag{4b}$$

The optimization

The optimization problem can be written as two Lagrange functions:

$$L(\tau_k, \tau_l, b) = c - \lambda(\tau_k f_k k + \tau_l f_l \bar{l} + \tau_c c + \gamma b - \varepsilon - \bar{g}) \tag{5a}$$

and

$$L(\tau_k^*, \tau_l^*, b^*) = c^* - \mu(\tau_k^* f_{k^*} k^* + \tau_l^* f_{l^*} \bar{l}^* + \tau_c^* c^* + \gamma^* b^* - \varepsilon^* - \bar{g}^*. \tag{5b}$$

where (5a) refers to the home country and (5b) to the foreign country.

Substituting (1a)/(1b) and (2a)/(2b) into (5a)/(5b), and calculating the derivatives of (5a) with respect to τ_k, τ_l, b and λ, and the derivatives of (5b) with respect to τ_k^*, τ_l^*, b^* and μ, equalizing them to zero and solving for the tax rates, yield the following:

$$f_l \bar{l}(1-\beta)[1-\delta\tau_c-(1-\delta)\tau_c^*]=0, \tag{6a}$$

which is particularly met when $\beta = 1$ (the domestic bonds are purchased only by residents) or when $\tau_c = \frac{1-\tau_c^*+\tau_c^*\delta}{\delta}$ and $\delta \neq 0$;

$$\begin{aligned}\frac{1-\delta\tau_c-(1-\delta)\tau_c^*}{f_{kk}(1-\beta\tau_c}\{(f_{kk}k+f_k)(\alpha(1-\tau_c)(1-\tau_k)+\beta[\tau_c+\tau_k(1-\tau_c)]) \\ +f_{kk}f_k k[(1-\tau_c)-\alpha]-(f^*_{k^*k^*}k^*+f^*_{k^*})(1-\tau_c)(1-\tau_k)(1-\alpha^*) \\ +f_{kl}\bar{l}(1-(1-\beta)[\tau_c+\tau_l(1-\tau_c)])\}=0\end{aligned} \tag{6b}$$

which describes the interdependences for capital taxation and;

$$\bar{g}+(1-\tau_c)[(\varepsilon-\gamma b)-\tau_k f_k k-\tau_l f_l \bar{l}]-\tau_c[(1-\tau_k)f_k k+(1-\tau_l)f_l \bar{l}]=0. \tag{6c}$$

The solution for the foreign country is symmetric to the one presented above. The system of equations (6a) – (6c) can be solved for a country but this time it provides an infinite number of results. This means that without taking into account the response of foreign country the taxes and bond issuance can be set in infinite number of ways. However, we can compute τ_k, τ_l, τ_k^* and τ_l^* from the formulas (6b) and (6c), with assumption that δ, δ^*, β, β^*, τ_c and τ_c^* fulfils the condition (6a). In this case there is only one solution for given set of parameters and the solution corresponds to Nash equilibrium. This equilibrium is vulnerable to the changes of parameters in both countries. Nevertheless the solution is unique but it is too complicated to be presented here. Instead of analysis of formula we formulate thesis on the result of numerical simulation. In basic version, if parameters of home and foreign country are the same then the tax rates are symmetric and the response of the equal changes of parameters is also symmetric. The analysis of the tax rates in the equivalence could be done only when other parameters stay fixed. Please note that τ_c and τ_c^* are either parameters in this approach, and we assume that they can be altered only when both countries would take the common action and the external obstacles for this policy would be removed. Technically we postulate the condition of (6a) to be met.

The formulas for equilibrium tax rates are not short and simple, so instead of algebraic derivation we provide numerical simulation, starting from the case of two symmetric countries and an increase in debt servicing in home country. The values used for simulation met the assumption of typical production function with decreasing marginal productivity of factors and positive cross-factor marginal effect (increasing labor or capital productivity in response of the changes of the second factor). The parameters are chosen so that the tax rates are similar to the average tax rates observed in the empirical sample used for econometric analysis. However the sample is only constructed for illustratory reason and it does not pretend to be the calibrated value taken of the real economy.

In the basic simulation involves the possession of home capital mainly by residents (0.9) whereas portfolio capital is possessed in lesser extend (0.7) than direct ones. The level of capital invested in the country and the marginal productivity of labor are chosen to obtain values of tax rates similar to the average level of tax rates on capital and labor in European countries used in econometric part of current study. This provides the equilibrium tax rates: $\tau_k^* = \tau_k = 0.34$ and $\tau_l^* = \tau_l = 0.24$.

Table 5: *Starting parameters of numerical simulation.*

$g=350$	$g^*=350$	$\beta=0.7$	$\beta^*=0.7$
$b=150$	$b^*=150$	$f_k=0.6$	$f_{k^*}^*=0.6$
$k=321.5$	$k^*=321.5$	$f_l=0.824$	$f_{l^*}^*=0.824$
$l=1200$	$l^*=1200$	$fk_k=-0.2$	$f_{k^*k^*}^*=-0.2$
$\varepsilon=350$	$\varepsilon^*=350$	$fk_l=0.04$	$f_{k^*l^*}^*=0.04$
$\alpha=0.9$	$\alpha^*=0.9$	$\delta=0.8$	$\delta^*=0.8$
$\gamma=0.9$	$\gamma^*=0.9$	$\tau_c=0.24$	$\tau_c^*=0.24$

Besides the calculation of tax rates in equilibrium we would like to know the reaction of tax rates on parameters referring to the debt. The formulas for τ_k, τ_l, τ_k^* and τ_l^* are explicit, so we can simply calculate the derivatives of the tax rates with respect to ε, b or γ. However it should be noted that γ and b affect the tax rates in the same way and opposite to ε, so it is not necessary to calculate all of derivatives. The most interesting for the crisis analyses are the derivatives of these four tax rates with respect to ε (debt servicing cost). The derivatives have the form of quotients and depend on the parameters of production function (particularly their first and second derivatives) and four parameters of the foreign share in capital and bonds (α, α^*, β and β^*). It should be emphasized that the latter group of parameter is restricted to the range $\langle 0;1 \rangle$ and determines the sign of tax rates changes triggered by changes of debt-servicing costs, if the production function has properties as assumed previously. This allow for the graphical presentation of result for the symmetric case when parameters of the ownership are the same in both countries (see Graph 1 and 2).

The quotient form of the four derivatives (τ_k, τ_l, τ_k^* and τ_l^*) means that there is a discontinuity of value (when the denominator of the quotient is zero), which splits all possible solution in two main regimes of tax rates changes. In first regime, $\alpha=\alpha^*$ and remains relatively low and $\beta=\beta^*$ is irrelevant or $\alpha=\alpha^*$ are high, and $\beta=\beta^*$ are high too. In the second regime, $\alpha=\alpha^*$ are high but $\beta=\beta^*$ are relatively low. The first regime represents the case of high direct investment internalization or the case of low direct and portfolio investment internalization (the situation close to autarky). The second regime is characterized by relatively low level of direct investment internalization (capital is mainly possessed by residents) and high level of bond portfolio internalization (the share of non-residents in the government bonds is relatively high). This regime is typical for developed open economies. In crises times the portfolio internalization should decrease relatively more than direct capital investment. Intuitively, during crises non-residents would reduce their foreign portfolio positions as they become to be viewed as more risky. However, the foreign direct investments are not greatly affected because they are not directly linked with the solvency of foreign government and they are not easy to liquidate without a sharp decline of value. The adjustment of tax rates on the debt parameters triggers a switch from the second regime to the first, with lower internalization of bonds portfolio. This alters the direction of tax rates change affected by debt servicing costs totally. The crisis can be then perceived as transitory return to less internalized economy (close economy) in the context of international investments.

It is worth of interest that the behavior of derivatives on capital and labor mirrors each others. This means that the reaction of tax rates in general works in opposite ways. The sensitivity of capital tax rates increases when the sensitivity of labor tax rates decreases. The situation can be shown on two graphs (Figures 21 and 22) where the first regime is on the left side of the discontinuity region (the area when derivatives increases or decreases rapidly – intersecting the graphs from south to north-east) and the second regime on the right side. The functional form of derivatives requires some parts of the derivative surface to be lying above and some parts – below. This means that direct tax adjustment have to be differentiated in respect of investment internalization level. This confirms that there is no universal pattern of tax rates adjustment forced by the changes of debt servicing costs. The changes are determined by the tax regime and the distance to the "discontinuity zone". Please note that reaction of tax rates on the debt-servicing-cost-change in both countries is asymmetric as a consequence of the increase only in one country (home) with foreign costs staying unaltered.

Figure 21. *The derivative of τ_k with respect of ε in the zero-one range when $\alpha = \alpha^*$ and $\beta = \beta^*$. First regime is on the left of the discontinuity region and second region on the right.*

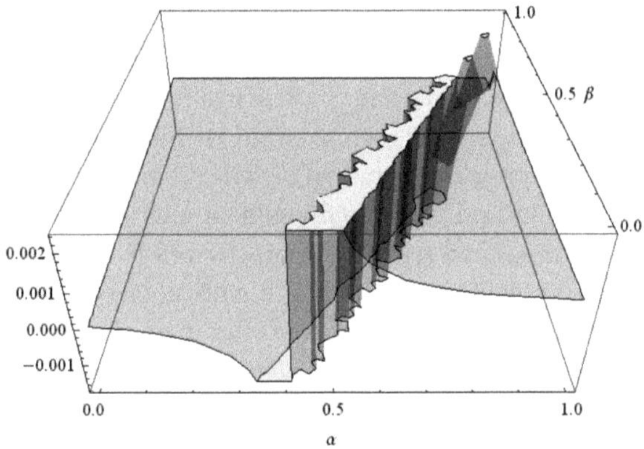

Source: Calculation in Mathematica 9

Figure 22. *The derivative of τ_l with respect of ε in the zero-one range when $\alpha = \alpha^*$ and $\beta = \beta^*$. First regime is on the left of the discontinuity region and second region on the right.*

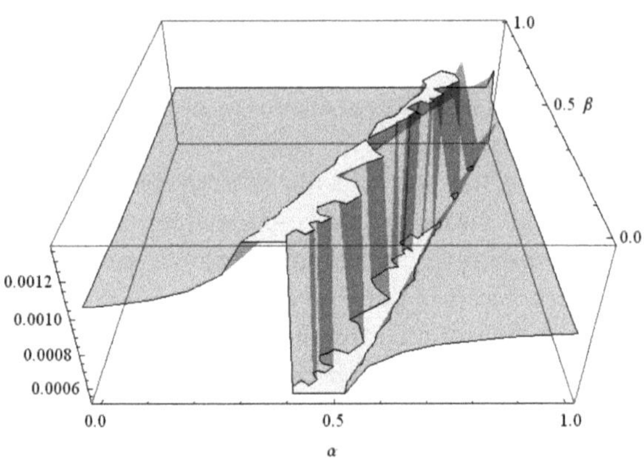

Source: Calculation in Mathematica 9.

The signs of the derivatives indicate that an increase of ε raises other tax rates except for τ_l^* (which decreases): $\frac{\partial \tau_k}{\partial \varepsilon} = 0.0011, \frac{\partial \tau_k^*}{\partial \varepsilon} = 0.00046, \frac{\partial \tau_l}{\partial \varepsilon} = 0.00079, \frac{\partial \tau_l^*}{\partial \varepsilon} = -0.00009$. This pattern is typical for the second regime. On average (looking for both-countries-tax-adjustment), this means that an increase in the one country debt servicing entails an increase in the capital tax rates but the effect on the average labor tax rates (calculated as average of labor taxes in both countries) is ambiguous. The country with debt problems has to increase the taxation of capital to get some money for enlarged repayment of debt. This encourages the same move of the country without debt problems because it lessens the tax completion. The home country affected by the higher servicing cost is forced to increase the labor taxation along with capital taxation but the foreign country need not to do that. Instead the labor taxation can be lowered because the solvency (of foreign country) is improving.

If the share of domestic ownership in capital declines, for example to $\alpha=\alpha^*=0.2$, then the tax adjustments should follow another pattern: $\frac{\partial\tau_k}{\partial\varepsilon}=0.00024, \frac{\partial\tau_k^*}{\partial\varepsilon}=-0.00042, \frac{\partial\tau_l}{\partial\varepsilon}=0.00096, \frac{\partial\tau_l^*}{\partial\varepsilon}=0.00008$. This is consistent with the first regime of tax rates adjustment. Now the average changes of the capital tax rates are ambiguous, and those of the labor tax rates are unequivocally positive. The labor tax rates react stronger than capital ones. The reaction of foreign labor tax is determined by the drop of foreign capital taxation. The latter is probably induced by the decrease of capital income received by foreign residents due to the capital income tax increase in the home country. The foreign government tries to attract capital to fulfill the drop of income which involves lower tax capital rates and higher taxation of labor. It should be noted that altering the betas does not affect the result significantly. Only for a very low β both tax rates on capital decrease in response to a change in ε. Slightly different but closer to what one would expect is an effect of ε on the tax rates when both pairs of $\alpha=\alpha^*$ and $\beta=\beta^*$ are relatively high (for example, if $\alpha=\alpha^*=0.8$ and $\beta=\beta^*=0.7$) In this case we obtain: $(\frac{\partial\tau_k}{\partial\varepsilon}=-0.00171, \frac{\partial\tau_k^*}{\partial\varepsilon}=-0.00238, \frac{\partial\tau_l}{\partial\varepsilon}=0.00135, \frac{\partial\tau_l^*}{\partial\varepsilon}=0.00046)$ Unfortunately the tax rates in this case drop beyond the reasonable range zero-one. In general, the border (the discontinuity) between the two regimes runs thereabout from $\alpha=\alpha^*=0.5$ and $\beta=\beta^*=0$ to $\alpha=\alpha^*=\beta=\beta^*=1$.

The above results are valid only if the consumption taxes are held constant. However, if both τ_c and τ_c^* increase then the taxes on capital and labor can be lowered, simply because the governments has another source of revenue. If we consider the situation with asymmetric debt (debt servicing rises in one country only), then higher taxation of consumption mitigates a part (or all) of a capital tax rate increase in the country with the solvency problem and stronger decreases the tax rate on capital in the other country (for first regime). The simulation results suggest that labor tax rates are expected to fall in both countries. This is consistent with hypothesis of substitutability between consumption taxation and labor taxation.

Summing up, an increase of consumption tax should be preferred by both governments when debt servicing grows (or when bonds issuance (b) or the discount rate (γ) decline), as it prevents a rise in taxes on capital and labor what usually happens during an economic crisis. Whether an effect on capital taxes is greater than an effect on labor taxes, and positive or negative, depends on the regime of tax rates changes, which is determined by the ratio of foreign and domestic investments in bonds and capital. Overreaction of foreign investors reducing positions in domestic government bonds with low reaction on capital market favors a switch from the second to the first regime. The latter means moderate changes of average capital tax rates and positive and higher changes of average labor tax rates during fiscal solvency crisis.

5. The new economic geography approach

Not everyone agrees that tax competition has a decisive impact on the capital taxation, especially in the face of ambiguous empirical research (Devereux, Griffith, Klemm, 2002; Devereux, Lockwood, Redoano, 2008; Winner, 2005; Bretschger, Hettich, 2005; Bénassy-Quéré, Gobalraja, Trannoy, 2007). One of the possible explanations of such results is the presence of suitably strong agglomeration effect, postulated by the school of new economic geography, overwhelming the tax competition effect. The former involves the growth of productivity of capital accumulated at the region as a kind of external effect (Baldwin, Krugman, 2004). In general traditional tax competition implies some kind of price competition (in the form of perfect competition or Bertrand oligopoly) without transportation cost, while closer to reality can be monopolistic competition with an important role of transportation cost. However, the latter form of competition requires identification of region with a greater concentration of capital (the core) and other regions with a low capital formation (peripheries). In the core, the capital concentration stimulates production by positive external effect despite the decreasing marginal productivity of capital. Therefore it could be cheaper to produce goods in the core and to sell it in peripheries, if transportation costs are not very high. On peripheries the positive effect of capital concentration is weak or absent because capital is dispersed (some models assume that all capital from peripheries will move to the core).

It should be emphasized that agglomeration effect does not imply increasing economies of scale at the level of individual companies. The increase of the productivity on a given region depends solely on the amount of already accumulated capital. The causes of agglomeration effects is the occurrence of benefits in cash and in kind, relating to, inter alia: the proximity of companies and institutions, elimination of inefficient enterprises by tightening competition, the emergence of specific business support services, and facilitated technology transfer in the core

(Baldwin, Krugman, 2004; Ottaviano, van Ypersele, 2005; Borck, Pflüger, 2006). The different capital endowment in regions is exogenous and it does not require detailed economical explanation (is treated as a stagnant). Obviously the existing capital equipment can be explained by various factors interacting in the past but these factors do not directly affect the current taxation so they can be omitted.

It is assumed that taxes are determined to ensure the maximization of social welfare in both regions. The additional productivity of capital in the core is similar to the rent (pure profit), so it can be taxed higher than on peripheries, providing the opposite result to the one predicted by the tax competition theory. The higher taxation in the core than at peripheries does not induce capital outflow, if agglomeration effect prevails the tax competition effect. The former one can force the tax rate increase in the core even above the efficient equilibrium level. This excessive capital taxation can be effective only if agglomeration benefits grow faster than productivity of capital falls. Otherwise, the effects associated with tax competition outweigh and tax is too low. In extreme cases, fear of loss of concentrated equity investments (agglomeration) can even lead to a stronger decline in capital taxation than in the absence of agglomeration effects (Fernández, 2005). As one can see this is especially difficult to falsify, because every kind of final effect can be attributed to the agglomeration effect (very high taxation as well as very low one). Nevertheless on the theoretical ground the agglomeration effect should lessen tax competition and the opposite prediction is less likely.

In ordinary case the taxes at peripheries remain low (or even zero because there could be no capital invested) to compensate the agglomeration disadvantage. Within the core tax competition can be explained by the traditional theory – when transaction costs inside the core are negligible – or also by competition of core-periphery type – if the latter are prominent. The persistency of the division on core and peripheries depends on the strength of agglomeration effect and the taxation applied in both regions. Only very high taxation of capital in the core can reverse the places of core and peripheries, destroying the production advantage of the former and commutating the characteristics of both regions. It is worth to notify that introduction of agglomeration forces to the competition analysis come back to the thesis formulated by Ch. Tiebout (1956), that not only tax burden is important but also the infrastructure that can be provided and financed by tax revenues.

Large countries located in the core do not compete for capital level with the net profitability of investment but they rather try to provide an advantage in business terms offered to potential investors. The sustainability of location advantage requires intensive tax financing, but in return gives the rent provided by extensive and centralized infrastructure. Taxes in the core can be higher because capital owners prefer to invest in locations with better infrastructure and do accept the higher taxation necessary for its maintenance. Intuitively, this means the occurrence of trade-off between higher level of taxation and better terms for production. As a result, the states located in the core can apply higher taxes, without fear of capital outflows and loss of welfare. This theory explains the occurrence of lower capital taxation in small countries located on the peripheries, regardless of their initial endowment in mobile production factors.

Only when capital is initially dispersed, the decline in trade costs (triggered by deepening economic integration) can lead to tax competition exacerbation and to the general decline of tax rates on capital, as predicted in traditional tax competition models. This is because competition forces are still present and taxes need not always be higher in the core than at the peripheries if agglomeration forces are not very strong. It does not exclude either the occurrence of equilibria in which the concentration of production did not occur, for example as a result of a dispersion effect (Baldwin, Okubo, 2009). This effect is based on the propensity of companies to locate away from their competitors in order to reduce competitive pressures incumbent upon them, resulting in a decrease of producer prices. The dominance of agglomeration effect over dispersion effect generally depends on the size of the company. The bigger it is, the more agglomeration effects outweigh the effect of dispersion, because the increase of enterprise size raises the cost advantage associated with the scale of production. In other words, large companies are more prone to market competition, if they obtain higher productivity after investment on a relatively large market.

Implementation the agglomeration effect into the model

Following Krogstrup (2004a) the agglomeration effect can be shown inside the tax competition model, assuming increasing productivity of capital with the level of capital accumulated in the country. Let's suppose that the increase of capital productivity is described by the function $h(k)$. The function is positive, its value is greater than one and it is indirectly dependent on the capital taxation level in the home country $h(k) \equiv h(k(\tau_k))>1$. For simplicity: the split between core and periphery is determined ex ante and agglomeration effect characterizes only home country. It means that $h^*(k^*) \equiv 1$ and there is no possible switch between the core and the periphery after taxation setting. From the investor point of view, the agglomeration effect is exogenous because an investor has no impact on the level of capital invested in the home country. Additionally the reaction of the capital productivity in agglomeration function on the capital taxation is assumed negative $\frac{\partial h(k)}{\partial \tau_k} < 0$. It is an equivalent that agglomeration effect decreases with capital taxation in home country because the value of invested capital is lowering with taxation. The agglomeration effect involves only capital because it is mobile and homogeneous. In contrast labor is assumed to be heterogeneous[14] and immobile which exclude the possibility of agglomeration in one of the countries. These assumptions modify the home country income:

$$y = (1-\tau_k)\alpha f_k kh(k) + (1-\tau_k^*)(1-\alpha^*)f_{k^*}^* k^* + (1-\tau_l)f_l \bar{l} + \beta(\varepsilon - \gamma b) + (1-\beta^*)(\varepsilon^* - \gamma^* b^*). \tag{7a}$$

and foreign country income:

$$y^* = (1-\tau_k^*)\alpha^* f_{k^*}^* k^* + (1-\tau_k)(1-\alpha)f_k kh(k) + (1-\tau_l^*)f_{l^*}^* \bar{l}^* + \beta^*(\varepsilon^* - \gamma^* b^*) + (1-\beta)(\varepsilon - \gamma b). \tag{7b}$$

The latter formula is altered because part of the home capital is possessed by foreigners (residents of foreign country). The description of consumption in the model (2a and 2b) remains valid but the equation for the current account equilibrium is slightly different:

$$\begin{aligned}&(1-\delta)y - (1-\delta^*)y^* \\ &= (1-\beta^*)(\varepsilon^* - \gamma^* b^*) + (1-\tau_k^*)\alpha^* f_{k^*}^* k^* - (1-\beta)(\varepsilon - \gamma b) \\ &- (1-\tau_k)\alpha f_k kh(k)\end{aligned} \tag{8}$$

Finally the budget constraint of home government is now equal to:

$$\bar{g} = \tau_k f_k kh(k) + \tau_l f_l \bar{l} + \tau_c c + \gamma b - \varepsilon, \tag{9}$$

because now capital income depends on the function of agglomerated capital.

Maximization of residents' consumption in both countries requires the replication of steps described in the basic models. The procedure provides the results which are similar to the obtained earlier in basic form of the model but asymmetric (because agglomeration effect affects only home country) and dependent on the values of two new values: $h(k)$ and $\frac{\partial h(k)}{\partial \tau_k}$. For the simulation with $h(k) = 1.01$ and $\frac{\partial h(k)}{\partial \tau_k} = -0.01$ and all other parameters from Table 1 the tax rates in equilibrium are: $\tau_k = 0.53$, $\tau_k^* = 0.41$, $\tau_l = 0.20$ and $\tau_l^* = 0.23$. As one can see the tax rates on capital are higher than in the case of pure tax competition and they are very vulnerable to the values of $h(k)$ and its derivative. The values used for simulation represent

14 However it should be noted that some studies postulate agglomeration effect for labor but not for capital (eg. Ludema, Wooton, 2000).

relatively low agglomeration effect but this effect highly enforce the level of tax rates in the equilibrium.

In general the higher absolute value of $h(k)$ and its derivative, the higher tax rates on capital in both countries. For example when $h(k) = 1.01$ and $\frac{\partial h(k)}{\partial \tau_k} = -0.02$ the tax rates changes to: $\tau_k = 0.67$, $\tau_k^* = 0.47$, $\tau_l = 0.17$ and $\tau_l^* = 0.22$, while $h(k) = 1.02$ and $\frac{\partial h(k)}{\partial \tau_k} = -0.01$ produces: $\tau_k = 0.57$, $\tau_k^* = 0.42$, $\tau_l = 0.19$ and $\tau_l^* = 0.22$. One can see two things: the higher taxation of capital the lower tax rates on labor in given country (there is substitutability of taxes on capital and labor) and the higher agglomeration effect the higher taxation in home country in comparison with the foreign country. The first effect is obvious because: higher capital taxation provides higher revenues for government which increase the solvency and the accumulation of capital is rising despite the higher taxation of capital income. As a consequence taxation on labor can be lowered without decrease of total tax revenues. The second effect is determined by the concentration of the capital in the core (home country). High productivity in the core allows for the higher taxation but in the same time the fear of capital outflow from periphery (here foreign country) does not allow for foreign country government to increase the taxation of capital in greater extend.

The sensitivity of tax rates on the change of debt servicing costs follows the same pattern of two regimes, known from the basic model. Therefore the direction of change depends on the tax regime and is exactly the same as in basic model. It should not be surprising, because basic model can be treated as the special case of the agglomeration effect model with $h(k) = 1$ and $\frac{\partial h(k)}{\partial \tau_k} = 0$. However the intensity of tax rates adjustment is different now. The magnitude of changes is decreasing with the value of $h(k)$ and increasing with the absolute value of the derivative $\frac{\partial h(k)}{\partial \tau_k}$. In the equilibrium, the high (in sense of high absolute value of $h(k)$) and slowly decreasing (small absolute value of $\frac{\partial h(k)}{\partial \tau_k}$) agglomeration effects stabilizes the tax rates changes (triggered by debt servicing costs), while small (low absolute value of $h(k)$) and rapidly deteriorating value of the agglomeration effect (high absolute value of $\frac{\partial h(k)}{\partial \tau_k}$) intensifies the other tax rates adjustment. Therefore in the world of agglomeration effects prevalence, the tax changes are moderate and taxes remain relatively high while in the simple "tax competition world" tax rates changes are high however the average taxation should be lower.

6. Transaction tax on bonds income

Countries can work together to reduce the impact of fiscal adjustments caused by phenomena related to debt. One of such a possibility is to tax the bond turnover by introduction of transaction tax or the tax imposed on the income of bonds. For example European Commission proposed the taxation of shares and bond turnover at rate 0,1% and derivative contracts at 0,01% (Pelster, 2013) if at least one side of transaction is EU's resident. On the one hand, such a policy can: provide the increase of tax revenues and facilitate the reduction of other tax rates[15], prevent the excessive speculation on the bond (debt) market and counteract the increase of debt servicing cost caused by the growing concerns of investors. At the same time transaction tax can allow for incidence of part of tax burden on non-residents, if they possess part of government securities issued, according to the hypothesis of tax burden export (Eijffinger & Wagner, 2002; Huizinga & Nielsen, 1997). On the other hand, transaction tax: reduces the attractiveness of government bonds acquisition, can lead to an increase in the taxation of labor and capital providing the increase of tax burden and inefficient allocation because of lower risk hedging (Pelster, 2014).

The transaction tax can be imposed on sales of bonds on primary or secondary market. The latter cannot be precisely described in the presented model because we do not distinguish shares from other form of direct investment but the effect of such taxation should be similar to the imposition of a tax on bonds issuance. The investors selling or buying bonds would receive less money which: could divert the turnover to other markets without tax or decrease the attractiveness of bonds return discouraging the attractiveness of bond purchase. In fact the transaction tax can involve three possibilities referring to the basic model: 1) the taxation of net income from debt servicing payments over the new purchases of bonds which is an equivalent of net income tax; 2) the taxation of debt servicing payments (but without taxation of bonds) which is similar to partial insolvency of the country or 3) the taxation of bond issuance (but without taxation of debt servicing costs) which is the most similar to the financial transaction tax recommended for EU but without involvement of shares or derivatives taxation. We are going to focus on the modeling of the first case in the first place as the most comprehensive one and to discuss the expected changes in capital and labor taxation for the cases 2 and 3. One thing should be pinpointed the common transaction tax is not the only possibility, because we can observe the unilateral action of one government

15 In the European Union the total tax revenue collected from this tax is counted at 35 billion euro per year (Stratfor, 2013).

or implementation of taxes with different rates in each country. Therefore the introduction of transaction tax can be harmonized or independent (Schäfer, 2012). In the latter case, it affects the balance of other tax rates in both countries. This requires the use of two rates of transaction tax – one for each country which greatly increase the number of considered scenarios.

Implementation of transaction tax to the model

We start with the basic model described by equations 1-6b with minor modifications. Introduction of transaction tax requires imposition of two other tax rates τ_b and τ_b^*. These two tax rates can be harmonized when $\tau_b = \tau_b^*$ or can be set separately by home and foreign country when $\tau_b \neq \tau_b^*$. We assume that new taxation would cover the income from bond issuance obtained by residents and non-residents in given country. The transaction tax is the only tax of this type of income, so there is no further income tax. The taxation revenue accrues to the government in the country issuing bonds. The tax cannot be avoided by investors as a withdrawing tax (paid at source). Similarly we assume that $\varepsilon - \gamma b > 0$ and $\varepsilon^* - \gamma^* b^* > 0$ (the bondholders from both countries are net receivers of income from bonds). The net income from bonds investments of home country residents is equal to:

$$(1-\tau_b)\beta(\varepsilon - \gamma b) \tag{10a}$$

and the foreign-country-residents' net income from investments in bonds should fulfill:

$$(1-\tau_b^*)\beta^*(\varepsilon^* - \gamma^* b^*) \tag{10b}$$

This modifies equations 1a and 1b in the part describing the income from bonds issuance. Moreover equation 3 (the balance of current account) takes now the altered form of:

$$\begin{aligned}(1-\delta)y - (1-\delta^*)y^* = (1-\tau_b^*)(1-\beta^*)(\varepsilon^* - \gamma^* b^*) + (1-\tau_k^*)\alpha^* f_{k^*}^* k^* - \\ (1-\tau_b)(1-\beta)(\varepsilon - \gamma b) - (1-\tau_k)\alpha f_k k,\end{aligned} \tag{11}$$

because we have to put the new taxes into the formula.

The new tax revenues accrue to the other budgetary revenues. This modifies the home government constraint to the following form:

$$\bar{g} = \tau_k f_k k + \tau_l f_l \bar{l} + \tau_c c + (1-\tau_b)(\gamma b - \varepsilon) \tag{12a}$$

The foreign budget constraint is set analogously as:

$$\bar{g}^{*} = \tau_k^{*} f_{k^{*}}^{*} k^{*} + \tau_l^{*} f_{l^{*}} \bar{l}^{*} + \tau_c^{*} c^{*} + (1 - \tau_b^{*})(\gamma^{*} b^{*} - \varepsilon^{*}) \quad 12b)$$

The optimization procedure is the same as before. The structure of the result for symmetric case can be characterized in following way – each tax rates is decreased or increased by the value of home transaction tax multiplied by a parameter and foreign transaction tax multiplied by another parameter. The signs of parameters depend on the type of tax rates and the type of the tax regime. For the second tax regime, tax rates on capital are decreased in both countries and labor tax rates are increased by foreign country transaction tax. In the case with parameters from Table 1 the total impact of transaction tax on home labor tax rates turn out to be negative because the parameter of home country transaction tax is higher than the parameter of foreign transaction tax. Precisely, using values from Table 1 (second regime) we obtain: $\tau_k = 0.34 - 0.24\tau_b - 0.1\tau_b^{*}$, $\tau_k^{*} = 0.34 - 0.24\tau_b^{*} - 0.1\tau_b$, $\tau_l = 0.24 - 0.17\tau_b + 0.02\tau_b^{*}$ and $\tau_l^{*} = 0.24 - 0.17\tau_b^{*} + 0.02\tau_b$. Therefore for 5% harmonized transaction tax (the high value of transaction tax is applied only for illustratory reason to pronounce the effect exerted on tax rates), the equilibrium tax rates on capital and labor would be about: $\tau_k = 0.32$, $\tau_k^{*} = 0.32$, $\tau_l = 0.23$ and $\tau_l^{*} = 0.23$. Therefore the transaction tax can be perceived as a tool jointly lowering tax burden on capital and labor but with higher effect on capital taxation.

One can note that unilateral tax on transactions unambiguously decreases capital tax rates in both countries. In the asymmetric case the labor tax rate is lower in the country introducing transaction tax and higher in the country without such a tax. However, we should remember the simulation does take into account neither the changes of the bonds volume purchases (b and b^{*} are constant) nor the debt servicing cost (ε). These parameters are assumed to be exogenous and out of control of policy-makers in the considered model. This can importantly affect the result because with constant demand for bonds transaction tax can be perceived as non-distortionary levy providing additional budgetary revenues without cost.

Referring to the previously distinguished two tax regimes, for the first of them, (e.g. when $\alpha = \alpha^{*} = 0.2$ and $\beta = \beta^{*} = 0.7$) – the transaction tax decreases both taxes on labor (home and abroad) but ambiguously affects capital tax rates[16]. Similar result is implied by high home share of direct and portfolio investment (like for

16 Sometimes, in the first regime, unilaterally set transaction tax can lower all home tax rates at the equilibrium but the more likely is the decrease of labor taxation and the increase of capital taxation (in simulation this occurs for instance when $\alpha = \alpha^{*} = \beta = \beta^{*} = 0.8$).

example: $\alpha = \alpha^* = 0.8$ and $\beta = \beta^* = 0.85$). This is especially interesting because during solvency crisis the internalization of government bond investments can decline significantly. Therefore, if we consider transaction tax as a remedy for solvency crisis then the potential effects of harmonized transaction tax should depend on the reaction of government bonds investment. Overreaction of foreign investors on solvency problem can switch the regime of tax rates adjustment from second to the first regime. In such a case lower level of bonds purchases by foreigners would induce decrease of labor taxation. In contrast, if foreign investors do not flee away, higher share of foreign portfolio investments would enhance the decrease of capital taxation[17].

Alternatively the transaction tax could be imposed either on debt servicing costs (ε) or on revenues from bonds (γb) only. The first case is an equivalent of the bailout and the second one is the same as a confiscation of the part of voluntary investment in bonds. These two types of taxation are extraordinary and hardly can be considered as a standard and persistent fiscal policy rules. Nevertheless, the (partial) bailout policy can be an interesting option for governments during the solvency crisis, so we can check their potential impact on other tax rates. It should be noted that structure of the results remains unaltered but the impact of transaction tax intensifies. For example, for the data from Table 1 transaction tax on epsilon provides: $\tau_k = 0.34 - 0.39\tau_b - 0.16\tau_b^*$, $\tau_k^* = 0.34 - 0.39\tau_b^* - 0.16\tau_b$, $\tau_l = 0.24 - 0.28\tau_b + 0.03\tau_b^*$ and $\tau_l^* = 0.24 - 0.28\tau_b^* + 0.03\tau_b$. Probably, the higher reaction could be explained by decline in the debt servicing cost and simultaneous growth of budget revenues.

If the tax is imposed only on bonds issuance then the formulas for capital and labor taxation turn out very complicated and sensitive to the value of parameters. For basic simulation from Table 1 (second regime) with $\tau_b^* = \tau_b = 0.05$ the following values represent equilibrium: $\tau_k = 0.03$, $\tau_k^* = 0.03$, $\tau_l = 0.29$ and $\tau_l^* = 0.29$. The new transaction tax greatly decreases taxation of capital which is at least partially covered by the higher taxation of labor. Switching to the first regime (when $\alpha = \alpha^* = 0.2$ and $\beta = \beta^* = 0.7$) completely changes results. Now transaction tax positively affects taxation of capital and negatively – taxation of labor. The first type of taxes reaches $\tau_k = \tau_k^* = 0.84$ and the second decreases significantly to $\tau_l = \tau_l^* = 0.13$. For $\alpha = \alpha^* = 0.8$ and $\beta = \beta^* = 0.85$ the tax rates are $\tau_k = 0.65$, $\tau_k^* = 0.65$, $\tau_l = 0.17$ and $\tau_l^* = 0.17$. Therefore once again the investment positions decide about the direction of transaction tax impact on capital and labor taxation. Unfortunately during crisis decreasing

17 This is consistent with the observation of Devereux (2003; 2008) that portfolio investments are necessary to finance direct investment.

internalization induces capital taxes to be higher and labor taxes to be lower. As before we can conclude that lower share of foreign investors makes the situation similar to closed economy when taxation of capital can be higher and labor should be not taxed.

7. Common tax base with formula apportionment

The harmonization of tax bases (introduction of common tax base) coupled with the assignment of income between different countries is one of the tax reforms that could counteract the negative effects of both tax competition and tax avoidance in European Union (Musgrave, 1972; Becker & Fuest, 2010a; Riedel & Runkel, 2007). According to this proposition the tax base can be harmonized in all countries under agreement and the tax base split between countries according to the true business activity of taxpayers. The one thing which appears as the most doubtful is the method of income assignment for individual countries (formula apportionment). The division of income requires the calculation of an enterprise consolidated tax base according to its true activity in different tax jurisdictions, taking into account the non-tax business characteristics, such as: sales, assets or employment. The side effect of this type of tax harmonization is the change of tax burden favoring countries with higher taxation. The distribution of tax revenues should decrease the tax burden on international businesses located in countries with higher taxation and increase in countries with low taxation simple because part of tax base would be assigned to countries with lower taxation. Without formula apportionment, the latter pay low taxes on all their income, including income realized in countries with high taxation. The formula apportionment can be introduced within the group of countries aimed at closer economic integration, such as the members of the European Union or Eurozone. Unfortunately, as long as these proposition can curb the tax avoidance within the Union, it also encourages in greater extend the use of tax benefits offered by third countries. It is especially evident if the consequence of such a policy would be an increase of the tax burden within the group o countries establishing a common tax base with formula apportionment.

The formula apportionment strives to hinder the possibility of income shifting between jurisdictions and it should closely reflect the scale of business operations in different countries. In theory the following factors measuring the activity of enterprises are considered as the proxy of true business activity of enterprises: assets, sales, employment, wages (payroll) or value added. Generally, the use of individual factors means their actual taxation. It stipulates that the income tax becomes de facto a tax on wages or sales after the introduction of common tax base but not a kind of capital taxation. In practice, this idea is applied in countries with a federal structure like: United States, Canada, or Switzerland. However the experiences of the formula apportionment are different. In most cases several different factors are accepted and different weights are used to determine the common tax bases per individual states or cantons. For example: in the United States the formula takes into account: assets, sales and payroll and the weights may not add up to unity; whereas in Canada only sales and payroll are applied with weights equal to ½ (Fuest, Hemmelgarn & Ramb, 2007; Szlęzak-Matusewicz, 2006). The choice of factors has the direct effect on the tax burden and it can be amplified or mitigated by the selection of weights.

It is believed in the literature that the most distorting factor is the use of wages in the formula. The wages are deducted from income hence it is sufficient to increase employment in low-tax countries to change the tax burden for the benefit of multinational enterprise (Altshuler & Grubert, 2010). The application of wages in the formula is justified only if the structure of inputs and their prices are fixed in the whole group of countries introducing the common tax base (Hellerstein & McLure, 2004). Otherwise, their use leads to a large distortion. Distortion concerns in particular countries at different levels of development, as well as business sectors, depending on their capital and labor intensity. Therefore, in the case of large wage differences between countries, it would be better to use labor as a measure of business activity, even though it imputes preferences for less developed countries in the group (Devereux & Loretz, 2008).

The use of sales is justified better, especially under destination principle (the taxation of goods in the place of their consumption). In the first instance, the amount of sales properly reflects market activity, while it should not be applied to factors generating pure profits (e.g. intellectual property or natural resources). The sale is also the most cumbersome from an administrative point of view, because it does not necessarily show the actual business processes and can be easily manipulated. For example, the question arises whether it should be counted sale of intermediate goods or only final goods or whether it should be calculated under origin or destination principle. The use of sales increases the tax burden imposed on enterprises and this discourages the sole application of sales in formula apportionment.

The value added exhibits some theoretical advantages, because: 1) it is not completely arbitrary but determined by the market; 2) it does not require the calculation of the cost of capital; 3) it can be used for any industry and 4) it is available to most taxpayers because it stands on the reporting of value added tax (VAT).

However, the value added[18] requires adjustment of wage cost, which should not be the basis for the income apportionment, as it relates to the labor and provides the real distortions. To get rid of labor costs for administrative reasons it can be difficult. Unfortunately, this factor is also prone to transfer prices manipulation in exports and imports. The other problems with this factor involve the adjustments for untaxed and tax-exempt activities, for example value-added-tax-exempt financial services (Mintz & Weiner, 2003). Financial services are frequently exempt from VAT because calculation of value added in their case is cumbersome and at least partially remains under control of financial institutions (for example banks can set prices on deposits and loans simultaneously producing the interest margin and as a result – the added value).

Three basic factors used to assign income (assets, wages and sales) were also the subject of theoretical investigation conducted to determine the best factor limiting the decline in the tax burden (Pethig & Wagener, 2007). Firstly, the more flexible the factor used in the formula apportionment is the lower tax rates can be expected. For this reason the factors most decreasing tax revenue are assets and the most inflexible and defending the tax base – sales. Secondly, taxation is too low when assets are used and they are excessively high with other factors (payroll or sales), if the labor is immobile. If the labor is mobile and government strives to maximize tax revenues, it is the best to use sales. It follows that in order to obtain an adequate level of tax revenues the different factors should be used jointly and they always should include assets and either wages or sales. The larger would the share of assets in the formula be, the lesser is the chance for excessive taxation. The results obtained by these authors cast some doubts on the omissions of conscious manipulation of sales volume. The latter can easily undermine the application of sales as a proxy of true business activity.

Unfortunately, the use of formula apportionment does not preclude the manipulation of the amount of tax base, for example, by modifying the volume of sales by fictitious purchases between companies from different countries. In

18 It is also postulated that it is better to calculate value added with the origin principle, which means that in contrast to the ordinary VAT based on destination principle, the value of imports and exports should be subtracted, and the value of investment should be added but without depreciation (Hellerstein & McLure, 2004). The calculation of value added with destination principle can lead to the disappearance of the part of value added. For example, if the whole production is exported and the recipient is not VAT taxpayer then the value added is not counted. To correct this one can need to run separate reporting on the destination of the exported goods, which makes this method more cumbersome than simple taxation of sales by the country of destination.

this context, the introduction of formula can even lead to the decline of welfare because in the new system the full taxation of pure profits (rent) is not possible, as a result of partial assignment of income to low-tax jurisdictions (Eggert & Schjelderup, 2003). In general the full taxation of pure profit is efficiency-improving because it allows for collection of tax revenues without making the distortion of production. The use of assets in the formula apportionment may encourage mergers with companies from low tax countries, while the use of wages can discourage such action (Gordon & Wilson, 1986). Similarly, despite the fact that intangible or financial assets contribute to the generation of enterprise's income, they are omitted in the formula of calculating a common tax base. This encourages tax arbitrage. For example, it could be profitable to carry out financial activities as a secondary activity of the international company, instead of holding it by independent financial institution. The income from productive activities would be taxed more leniently because of the income apportionment to low-tax countries, which is not possible in the case of financial services where the term "volume of sales" is hard to assess. Another example of arbitrage can be the use of sales agent positioned in a low-tax country. Sales for such an agent would accrue to the income generated in low-tax country and it would decrease the total tax burden. In contrast, the agent may not report any taxable income, making further sales of the purchased goods to the country of high taxation (Altchuler & Grubert, 2010). Based on the above examples, the opponents of the formula apportionment argue that the introduction of common tax base can result only in changes of tax avoidance patterns but it would not eliminate the problem of income shifting between jurisdictions. In the new system of common tax base, taxpayers would concentrate on the correction of factors used to assign income to individual jurisdictions instead of correction of gain, as it is in the current system of separate calculation of tax bases.

In fact, there is a consensus that formula apportionment leads to lower corporate taxation, especially if the participation in the system remain voluntary (i.e. applied only by companies that want to accede), the tax rate is set by countries separately or the introduction of new system is accompanied by an international consolidation of losses. In particular the latter conclusion is confirmed by one of the recent developments in this field (Nielsen, Raimondos-Møller & Schjelderup, 2010). The authors indicated that the effectiveness of application of the formula apportionment depends on the cost of transfer prices and the amount of pure profit (rent) generated by an international enterprise. For the low level of pure profit (or very high) and the average cost of transfer pricing, the proposed reform would reduce the amount of tax revenue collection. This advocates for the abandonment of formula apportionment from policy practice. However the opposite conclusion was argued in (Kind, Midelfart-Knarvik & Schjelderup, 2005). The formula apportionment should reduce the sensitivity of the transfer pricing to the tax rates changes, in comparison to the separate (not-consolidated) accounting. As a result, countries with formula apportionment would be able to set higher taxes than others. Nevertheless the cited studies do not refer to the possibility of factors manipulation included in the formula, for example such as sales.

It should be also noted that the reallocation of capital caused by taxation is higher in the case of formula apportionment than in the case of income calculated with traditional method (Gordon & Wilson, 1986; Mintz, 2004; Altshuler & Grubert, 2010). There is not good news from the point of view of harmful tax competition prevention, because it triggers the increase of the capital mobility. Increasing tax competition as a result of application of the formula apportionment could be also explained in another way (Gordon & Wilson, 1986). Usually taxation of capital causes the capital outflow and increases the profitability before tax. However, in the case of formula apportionment the part of tax revenues goes abroad. Therefore, governments are not willing to tax capital high which exacerbated underfunding of public goods. Yet another explanation states that attracting additional capital by low taxation is profitable for the government. Such a policy increases country's total tax revenue share in the group of countries applying common tax base because it simultaneously increases revenue of labor taxation and induces an increase of sales. These two effects outweigh the revenue reduction induced by lower taxation of capital. Obviously, since all competing countries behave in the same way, the collected tax revenue has to decrease and the total amount of funds for distribution in the group of countries is lower (Sørensen, 2004).

The simulation of financial and economic results caused by the introduction of common tax base with formula apportionment is ambiguous. For example, the introduction of common tax base combined with the consolidation of subsidiaries and companies' losses would result in a decrease or increase in tax revenues, depending on the nature of participation in the new system of taxation. The consolidation means the summation of all incomes and losses from European Union's units forming an international company. In the case of voluntary participation, the total decline in tax revenues of European Union countries would be on average of 2.5%, however for some countries (Slovakia, Czech Republic, Hungary) the tax revenues can be higher (Devereux & Loretz, 2008). In the case of compulsory participation, assuming unchanged profitability and constant tax rates, the revenues should increase by about 2%. The effects of common tax base spill unequally on the country level, some countries could gain significantly (e.g. Spain), while others would record the decline of tax revenues (e.g. Finland). There are also studies referring to the enterprise level. The predictions based on disaggregated data show higher differences in estimated tax revenues than those provided only on international level. Much higher drop – reaching 22% of corporate income tax revenues – has been estimated in the study of German multinationals (Fuest, Hemmelgarn & Ramb, 2007). The basic reason for this effect was the consolidation of losses. The separate use of formula apportionment (without consolidation of losses) should cause shift of the tax revenues between small and large countries of the European Union, favoring the situation of the latter. However some small countries could either expect the increase of tax revenues. In the "winners" group of small countries were: Austria, Greece and Portugal. The probable cause of much higher drop in tax receipts in this study was the assumption of immediately deductible loss, while the current tax regulations allow for deductions of losses for several years or even prohibit the deduction in one year (e.g. in Poland, the yearly deduction cannot be higher than 50% of the losses from the previous year).

It should be added that quite opposite results were obtained for American multinationals (Shackelfors & Slemrod, 1998) where the formula apportionment including equal shares of assets, sales and payroll was investigated. The authors pointed out the possibility of tax revenues increase by about 38% on average and up to more than 80% for oil companies. This astonishing result is a consequence of disproportionately small share of domestic operations relatively to the foreign ones for American enterprises. As the authors speculate this may be caused by the one of three reasons: 1) the higher profitability of foreign activities, 2) the transfer of profit-motivated avoidance or 3) the occurrence of errors in the financial data. The high level of growth in tax revenues after the imposition of the formula apportionment can be achieved with respect of two assumptions: unchanged behavior of multinational companies and the omission of delayed profits repatriation from foreign subsidiaries. Especially this last factor may significantly overstate the benefits of the formula apportionment. The inclusion of behavioral adaptations, raise some doubts about the advantage of formula apportionment over separate accounting method (Altshuler & Grubert, 2010).

On the other hand, based on the expected economic impact of the common consolidated tax base introduction on economic growth (Kutarba, 2011), the increase of GDP can be expected only in five European Union countries: Belgium, Malta, Germany, Luxembourg and Italy. Other countries would lose on this but the losses should be moderate. For example Poland would lose about 1% of GDP, while the greatest losses of all analyzed countries would incur Ireland (3% of GDP).

It is also not entirely clear whether the use of a common tax base would reduce the tax audit. After the introduction of common tax base with formula apportionment, the benefits of tax audit are shared with other countries in contrast to country tax systems with only national tax audit. The split of tax revenues between many countries can discourage the intensity of control efforts on the country level, because it lowers financial incentives of the audit (the control effort in part works on the behalf of foreign budgets). Obviously the reaction of tax control is reversed in the absence of tax base harmonization, because the opportunity of tax burden shifting to foreign entities encourage the higher than optimal (excessive) tax audit[19]. The combined effect of the tax rates increase and a decline of tax audit is not determined a priori. The listed arguments suggest the need for centralization of tax audit at the supranational level, in the case of the implementation of a common tax base with formula apportionment, to prevent the tax base erosion.

Application of formula apportionment to the model

The idea of formula apportionment requires the application of common budget constrain for both countries in the model. Therefore the governments' constraints are different from the presented in formulas 4a and 4b, because now the tax revenue from capital is calculated together for both countries and then multiplied by the home-country-share parameter u. The u is responsible for the part of capital income tax accruing to home country budget and is predetermined by the chosen form of formula apportionment. The government constraint of home country takes the form:

$$\bar{g} = u(\tau_k f_k k + \tau_k^* f_{k^*} k^*) + \tau_l f_l \bar{l} + \tau_c c + \gamma b - \varepsilon, \tag{13a}$$

Like before, we assume that f_{k^*} and k^* in equation 13a are vulnerable to the changes of home capital, triggered by the home taxation of capital. Precisely $f_{k^*} = f_{k^*}[K - k(\tau_k)]$ and $k^* = [K - k(\tau_k)]$. K stands for the total amount of capital available in both countries at the moment. The foreign government constraint is similar to the presented above for home country:

$$\bar{g}^* = (1-u)(\tau_k f_k k + \tau_k^* f_{k^*} k^*) + \tau_l^* f_{l^*} \bar{l}^* + \tau_c^* c^* + \gamma^* b^* - \varepsilon^*. \tag{13b}$$

Respectively for 13b, the marginal productivity of capital and the amount of capital in home country are affected by taxes of foreign country: $f_k = f_k\ [K - k^*\ (\tau_k^*)]$

19 This is consistent with the export of tax burden hypothesis (Huizinga & Nielsen, 1997). In this case, there is no incidence on foreign investors but the tax audit is tighter for nonresidents than for residents.

and $k^* = [K - k^*(\tau_k^*)]$. The share of foreign budget in total income tax revenues is just a complement of home share to 1. The rest components of the basic model are not altered.

One can investigated three different cases of formula apportionment. In the first: the $u = \frac{k(\tau_k)}{K}$, so the tax revenues are divided between countries according to the capital invested in countries (recalling that $K = k + k^*$). In the second case: $u = \frac{f_l \bar{l}}{f_l \bar{l} + f_{l^*} \bar{l}^*}$, which means that the split of revenues is driven by ratio of the remuneration of employees in given country to the total remuneration of labor in both countries. In this setting, we can omit the problem of choosing the apportionment on the tax-sensitive-amount of capital. Instead we can concern on the product of fixed labor and its productivities which are only indirectly affected by capital taxation (capital tax rates affect the amounts of capital in both countries and this moderates the marginal productivities of labor). Finally, we can use constant multipliers (for example, capital ratio) but assuming that this share is not tax-driven (it is not optimized) and remains exogenous to the agents: $u = \frac{k}{K}$. In the last proposition capital for the calculation of the income split is fixed and taken from past. This does not preclude the tax competition but remains simpler to implementation by tax authorities (governments).

The optimization process leads to a unique Nash-equilibrium solution of tax rates and the numerical simulation produces the result that can be compared with the result of basic model. In the first case, (formula apportionment with capital invested) the basic simulation of optimal tax rates when ($\alpha = \alpha^* = 0.9$ and $\beta = \beta^* = 0.7$) provides the following tax rates: $\tau_k = -0.24$, $\tau_k^* = -0.24$, $\tau_l = 0.35$ and $\tau_l^* = 0.35$. The tax rates are symmetric but the negative sign of capital taxation is unexpected. It means the capital should be subsidized – not taxed in the equilibrium. This result undermines the idea of formula apportionment as a remedy for harmful capital tax competition, because after the imposition of such a formula, the taxation of capital is not higher in both countries but even it turns out to be negative. The most probable explanation of this result refers to the theory of optimal capital taxation. Higher level of accumulated capital increases the productivity of labor and the higher taxation of the latter mitigates the problem of setting positive tax rates on capital in both countries. In other words both countries cooperate in maximizing the revenues from labor and they use capital taxation as a tool to achieve this objective. Therefore the common budget constraint induces governments to promote the accumulation of capital and indirectly to enhance the productivity of labor. The side effect of such a policy covers the higher taxation of labor if we compare this case with the situation of separate budget constraints. In the new equilibrium the additional part of labor tax revenues is required to finance the greater subsidization of capital. The results for relatively high and similar home share of direct and portfolio investment ($\alpha=\alpha^*=0.8$ and $\beta=\beta^*=0.85$) (referring to the first regime when the internalization of direct and portfolio investments are low) provides even higher level of capital subsidization and higher taxation of labor: $\tau_k=-0.48$, $\tau_k^*=-0.48$, $\tau_l=0.40$ and $\tau_l^*=0.40$.

The reaction of tax rates on the changes of ε (from 350 to 380) when ($\alpha=\alpha^*=0.9$ and $\beta=\beta^*=0.7$) produces following values of tax rates: $\tau_k=-0.23$, $\tau_k^*=-0.25$, $\tau_l=0.38$ and $\tau_l^*=0.35$. The result for ($\alpha=\alpha^*=0.8$ and $\beta=\beta^*=0.85$) are: $\tau_k=-0.47$, $\tau_k^*=-0.48$, $\tau_l=0.43$ and $\tau_l^*=0.40$. The tax subsidization on capital decreases in the country with debt problem irrespectively of the regime type. The subsidization of capital in foreign country slightly increases (in the second regime) and the taxation of labor is roughly constant. The tax on labor increases in home country as a reaction of worsening solvency.

Obviously it cannot be excluded that capital formula apportionment is not appropriate, because tax competition concern is strictly focused on capital movements. For this reason, in the second case the formula based on the capital is replaced with the one based on labor remuneration. Unlike the previous formula, this one requires finally the determination of two new derivatives values: $\frac{\partial f_{l^*}}{\partial \tau_k}$ and $\frac{\partial f_l}{\partial \tau_k^*}$ which have been absent in the capital formula. The signs of both these derivatives are expected to be positive because higher capital taxation in one country increases the capital level in the second country and the latter stimulates the labor productivity (and wages) in the last. For simulation we assume these two derivatives to be equal each other with value of 0.1. The last assumption provides the tax rates in symmetric equilibrium (for the basic simulation parameters when $\alpha=\alpha^*=0.9$ and $\beta=\beta^*=0.7$) to be equal to: $\tau_k=-0.18$, $\tau_k^*=-0.18$, $\tau_l=0.34$ and $\tau_l^*=0.34$. One can notice these values to be consistent with values obtained in capital formula apportionment although slightly lower in absolute term. The different level of direct and portfolio investment typical for less open economies ($\alpha=\alpha^*=0.8$ and $\beta=\beta^*=0.85$) increases the level of capital subsidization and the taxation of labor: $\tau_k=-0.31$, $\tau_k^*=-0.31$, $\tau_l=0.37$ and $\tau_l^*=0.37$. As one can see, the general pattern of tax rates in equilibrium is unchanged. It should be emphasized that despite the slightly lower capital subsidization (in both cases) than in the case of capital investment formula, this case is not comparable with the previous one because it depends on the values of two additional parameters (the derivatives of marginal productivities of labor at home and abroad).

Increasing debt servicing cost in home country ε alters the tax rates and the level of capital subsidization. For example, when $\alpha=\alpha^*=0.9$ and $\beta=\beta^*=0.7$ and the ε in home country increases to 380 (from 350), then tax rates in equilibrium set out to: $\tau_k = -0.16$, $\tau_k^* = -0.19$, $\tau_l = 0.37$ and $\tau_l^* = 0.34$. Respectively when $\alpha = \alpha^* = 0.8$ and $\beta = \beta^* = 0.85$ then the new tax rates would be: $\tau_k = -0.29$, $\tau_k^* = -0.32$, $\tau_l = 0.40$ and $\tau_l^* = 0.36$. Similarly, in the case of formula apportionment on invested capital, changes stay in line with expectations because the capital subsidization decreases in country with higher debt servicing costs and the taxation of labor increases. The labor taxation in country without such a problem slightly decreases and the subsidization of capital rises. It should be pinpointed that common budgetary constraint makes the direction of changes coherent irrespectively of the regime of tax rates changes and the method of formula apportionment.

In the last case, the ratio of capital invested at home (abroad) is treated as constant and by assumption does not react to the tax rates changes. (It does not mean capital investment becomes inelastic to the tax changes but only that tax authorities choose the share of income split with constant parameter). For a basic set of fiscal values and the second regime ($\alpha = \alpha^* = 0.9$ and $\beta = \beta^* = 0.7$) the tax rates are: $\tau_k = -0.24$, $\tau_k^* = -0.24$, $\tau_l = 0.35$ and $\tau_l^* = 0.35$. When $\alpha = \alpha^* = 0.8$ and $\beta = \beta^* = 0.85$ then the new tax rates are equal to: $\tau_k = -0.48$, $\tau_k^* = -0.48$, $\tau_l = 0.40$ and $\tau_l^* = 0.40$. Comparing with the first case (endogenously chosen level of invested capital) the result is very similar. Exactly we observe slightly higher subsidies to capital and higher taxation of labor in the last case (but these effects are smaller than one percent point).

Finally, altering the debt servicing cost to 380 we can notice the change of equilibrium tax rates. For basic case of $\alpha = \alpha^* = 0.9$ and $\beta = \beta^* = 0.7$ the rates are: $\tau_k = -0.23$, $\tau_k^* = -0.25$, $\tau_l = 0.38$ and $\tau_l^* = 0.35$. When $\alpha = \alpha^* = 0.8$ and $\beta = \beta^* = 0.85$ the rates are close to: $\tau_k = -0.47$, $\tau_k^* = -0.48$, $\tau_l = 0.43$ and $\tau_l^* = 0.40$. Calculated tax rates in equilibrium perfectly match results obtained for the formula apportionment when invested capital is treated as endogenous.

Summing up, all the considered cases have similar characteristic, providing the subsidization of capital together with taxation of labor in the equilibrium. The reaction of increasing debt servicing cost is standardized because capital subsidization decreases in countries experiencing debt problems and this allows for increasing capital subsidization in country without such a problem. The increasing budgetary needs are covered by the increase of labor taxation in the home country (by assumption the country with debt problems) and do not change the taxation of labor in foreign country. The increasing subsidization of capital in foreign country is financed by the capital inflow due to the decreasing subsidization of capital in the home country.

Chapter 3
Dynamic model of fiscal solvency with capital tax shifting

1. Introduction

Optimization is crucial in economic analysis. For this reason, calculus methods of solving unconstrained and constrained optimization problems occupy an important place in economist's tool kit. Such methods are applicable frequently to static optimization problems, where the solution usually consists of a single optimal value for every choice of variables. Nevertheless the static model is very useful in the simulation of short term fiscal policies but falls short in the description of long term behavior of taxpayers and governments. Forward looking economic agents recognize that decisions made today influence those to be made in the future. Today's decisions may expand or contract the set of admissible choices in the future by raising or lowering their cost. Such intertemporal linkage is embedded in dynamic optimization processes in economics. That's why mathematical methods that account for such connections are fundamental to economic decisions. A dynamic optimization states the question about the optimal magnitude of a choice variable in each point of time. It also allows for considering an infinite planning horizon. The solution to the dynamic optimization problem takes the form of an optimal time path for every choice variable. The latter requires the maximization of discounted government revenue in the long-term equilibrium.

Therefore, to shed some light to this issue, we develop a dynamic optimization model of one-country government maximizing the revenue of taxes and bonds. Optimal Control Theory and the Maximum Principle have been developed by Lev S. Pontryagin (Pontryagin, 1962) and they will be used in this chapter to solve the dynamic optimization problem of finding optimal fiscal policy for government having three tax rates and the revenue from bonds issuance constrained by solvency rule. It should be noted that this equilibrium is one country equilibrium and cannot be extended to include interaction with other country or group of countries, like Nash equilibrium in the static model presented in the previous chapter. This excludes the calculation of equilibria sensitive to the value of parameters from second country but does not preclude the analysis of the changes of tax rates in equilibrium induced by the changes of selected parameters.

In optimal control problems, variables are divided into two classes, namely the state (or phase) variables and the control variables. The evolution of the state variables is dictated by the control variables, via a set of differential equations which describe the dynamics of the state variables. Further, the control as well as the state variables are generally subject to constraints, which make problems in optimal non-classical control, since problems with path constraints can hardly be solved by the application of classical method of dynamic optimization i.e. calculus of variations. The formulation of an optimal control problem requires several steps: the choice of the class of admissible controls, the mathematical description of the system to be controlled, the specification of a performance criterion (the goal function) and constraints that should be satisfied. A nontrivial part of dynamic optimization problem is the modeling of state variables. The objective of the procedure is to obtain the simplest mathematical description that correctly predicts the response of the state variables to all admissible controls (the state equation). We shall restrict our considerations to the system of ordinary differential equations in phase space form:

$$\dot{x}(t) = f(t, x(t), u(t)) \tag{1}$$

Here $t \in R$ stands for the independent variable (time), vector for state variables and vector $u(t)$ for the control variables. State variables characterize the behavior of the system at any time instant t, whereas control variables represent input or manipulated variables at time t. A solution to this state equation is called a response of the system, corresponding to the control $u(t)$. It will be assumed that function f is continuous in the variables t, x, u and continuously differentiable with respect to x.

A performance criterion, the goal function, must be specified to evaluate the performance of the system quantitatively. In this chapter, we shall use the following objective function:

$$\int_0^\infty R(t, x(t), u(t)) e^{-\rho t} dt \tag{2}$$

This is an integral from zero to infinity of the objective function with respect of time. The function under integral is discounted to avoid the infinity in the solution of the problem. Having defined an objective function, the set of state equations and the set of admissible controls, we can state the optimal control problem as follows: find an admissible control $u^*(t)$ which satisfies state equations in a manner providing the maximum value of goal function.

When we solve static optimization problem the choice of optimal decision is made just one time. There is no planning for the future, nor are the future decisions to be made in static optimization problem. This is exactly what the static framework of the problem dictates. In contrast the solution to the dynamic optimization problem is a time path of optimal decisions over the relevant planning horizon. The time path of optimal decisions maximizes the objective function. The model differs visibly from static approach presented before in several points.

Firstly, the maximization concerns revenues not the utility or private consumption. Thereby it is better suited to the behavior of Leviathan-type government. Such approach helps to set the maximum tax burden available in the long term which can be necessary to sustain fiscal solvency. Nevertheless, taxation cannot be too high because this could diminish the tax base and a lower tax base limits the maximum level of bonds issuance. The choice of utility as an optimization criterion can produce solutions with very low taxation which is not typical to the solvency problems. In other words the analysis assesses the maximum tax burden which can be levied on society to fulfill the repayment needs. Nevertheless the connection between tax revenue and tax base requires taxation to be set at relatively moderate level.

Secondly, the maximization involves three tax rates (defined as control variables) because the value of bonds is determined by the tax revenue and tolerance of the market to the proportion of tax revenues to the production. The parameter of the tolerance affects the possibilities of borrowing on the market but in general its value in the long term should be invariable. Introduction of the tolerance measure prevents the needs of financial market modeling and eliminates the interest rate calculation. Technically the constraint imposed on the borrowing of government excludes the solution with infinitive bonds issuance (because voluntary indebtedness is less harmful than compulsory taxation, the infinite bonds issuance is preferred in the optimization process) and allows for positive level of debt in the equilibrium instead of zero. Sometimes the zero indebtedness is postulated in the long term because if the value of debt is positive then the some part of lenders does not receive the repayment for the previously purchased bonds. The proposition adopted in the dynamic model deals with this problem postulating only partial repayment of the debt in the long term and prevents to treat the debt as a transitory phenomenon.

Thirdly, the dynamic setting assumes that there is no reaction of other country on tax rates in home country because analysis is made only from one side. This eliminates the inflow of foreign income from consideration. But this requires the introduction of mechanism inducing effects similar to tax competition from other country. Therefore tax competition manifests itself in two aspects: the capital income shifting possibility specified by the value of parameter s (similar to the concept incumbent in the one country static model) and with the share of explicit consumption a. The last parameter divides total consumption into two parts. The greater part is explicit and taxed with consumption tax and the smaller part is implicit and avoids taxation. Precisely the implicit consumption $(1 - a)$ measures the size of shadow economy and puts some restrictions on the maximum available consumption tax. Without this restriction it could be preferable for government to set taxes on consumption at 100% level and then redistribute all revenues between consumers. This would be most likely because consumption taxation provides fewer distortions than taxes on capital and labor. It should be noted that in dynamic setting capital and consumption are state variables and their level cannot be treated as fixed even in the final equilibrium.

Fourthly, labor is endogenous and depends on the dynamics of labor force creation and the income effect of labor taxation. Taxes levied on labor enhance the labor supply growth because people try to compensate the decrease of income caused by taxation. Simultaneously the substitution effect is negligible because consumer does not possess additional assets, so they cannot give up they work. The strength of tax income effect is captured by positive parameter h reflecting the formation of human capital.

Fifthly, the dynamic optimization extends the prediction to infinite time. In such a framework bonds can be considered as savings which was impossible in the one-period static model. The infinite solution provided by dynamic model can be helpful rather in understanding the ultimate levels of taxation than changes induced by current economic policy. However the dependence paths can be very informative in relation with reactions observed in short-term. Obviously it cannot be excluded that some tax would work in opposite direction in short and long term because of different objective (utility versus revenue maximization) or because of more flexible adjustment occurring in longer period.

2. The model

Government maximizes the revenues consisting of tax receipts of: explicit consumption ac, capital income available in country srk, remuneration of labor wl and bonds issuance b. We assume that only part of total consumption is known for the tax authorities, so there is a shadow economy equal to $(1 - a)c$. The capital is paid with interest rate r and the part $(1 - s)$ of capital income avoids taxation (because domestic capital is hidden or it can escape abroad). These two parameters are exogenous and fixed over time because we assume constant "avoidance technology" available for all taxpayers in the long term. The income of labor is explicit and calculated as labor multiplied by the wage. Finally the bonds issuance is simply equal b. Therefore we do not use the discount factor or debt servicing costs in the model. The objective of government is the sum of previously described revenues:

$$\tau_c ac + \tau_k srk + \tau_l wl + b \tag{3}$$

where c, k and l are state variables in the dynamic optimization nomenclature.

The first three elements of equation (3) describe the tax revenues. Consumption is divided into explicit (taxable) and implicit (untaxed). The share of these two sets of consumption specifies the parameter a – defined as the size of a taxable part of consumption. The consumption tax rate is τ_c, while $1 - a$ is the part of consumption that is done in the shadow economy or abroad and therefore remains untaxed. For the purpose of optimization, we assume that a is a constant and has a value in the range from 0.5 to 1 to ascertain the value of τ_c to be in range 0-1. In the further numerical analysis changes of this parameter will allow to determine how the different opportunities of consumption taxation (e.g. tax base broadening or limitation of shadow economy) can affect the other rates of taxation and the equilibrium level of bonds. Income from capital is taxed at the rate τ_k. Alike in the case of consumption, only part of the capital income is taxed and the rest is hidden or transferred abroad. The size of the transferred or concealed income is described by the shifting parameter s. The s remains in the range of 0-1, while the value of 1 means no income shifting and 0 a full shifting. In practice, this can cover the broad range of phenomena such as: hiding income, limitation imposed on income transfer abroad, tax exemptions or legal form of income tax reduction. Finally, labor income is taxed with a rate τ_l. The labor is considered immobile and the labor income is explicit which means that it cannot escape the labor tax. The labor income is counted as the wage w multiplied by l. There is no unemployment in the economy.

Control variables in the model are, respectively, the tax rates on consumption τ_c, capital τ_k and labor τ_l. We allow only for solutions with tax rates satisfying the following condition: $0 \leq \tau_c, \tau_k, \tau_l \leq 1$. This excludes the possibility of consumption, capital or labor subsidization sometimes postulated in optimal taxation models and eliminates the models with tax rates exceeding 100% or with imaginary numbers. The subsidization involves negative tax rates on some control variables. The proposed constraint removes from the set of possible outcomes the boundary solutions with one of tax rates equal 100%. Obviously negative or 100% taxation is not adhering to the real world especially in the long term[20].

Apart from taxes the government can issue bonds. The debt financing is superior to the tax revenues because it does not produce distortions to the economy, like taxes levied on factors of production or consumption. However, the size of bonds issuance is not arbitrary. We assume that the level of new bonds is determined on the financial market and requires fulfilling the prespecified relation between tax revenues and the amount of production. The realization of this condition is an equivalent of fiscal solvency rule. Since the production function in equilibrium is not known (it depends, among others, on the relation between labor and capital and technological progress), we assumed that it could be substituted by the product of labor and capital as a proxy of the production. Accordingly, the greater is bonds issuance, the higher the tax revenues in relation to the product of capital and labor. In other words, the new debt level depends positively on the relation similar to the rate of fiscalism – the relation between tax revenue and production. Nevertheless in contrast to the rate of fiscalism we augmented the formula with non-negative parameter p - the tolerance for indebtedness. The latter is defined as the sensitivity of the financial market to the fiscal solvency condition. The magnitude of this parameter determines the level of new bonds issuance under current circumstances. This assumption simplifies investor reaction modeling in the long term by exclusion of the interest rate impact and the capacity of the financial market. Finally, the restriction on the new debt (bonds issuance) takes the following form:

$$b_t = p\frac{a\tau_c c + \tau_l wl + \tau_k srk}{k\,l}, \quad p \geq 0 \tag{4}$$

where $c, l, k > 0$, which enforces positive amount of: consumption, labor and capital. This constraint precludes the situation when the level of bonds in the equilibrium goes to infinity or zero. Both cases seem to be unpractical and concern the lack of proper risk assessment by the investors or the infinite capacity of the financial market. Simultaneously, (4) is consistent with the observation that poor

20 In the short term some solutions predicted negative tax rates. For example, compare the result obtained for the imposition of financial transaction tax with negative taxation of capital. Nevertheless these were solutions of Nash equilibrium between two countries providing coherent fiscal policy with different tax rates and bonds issuance. In dynamic model we have only one country, so we can look for cooperative or non-cooperative equilibrium with other countries. In this case we could not explain the negative taxation as the ultimate purpose of government maximizing revenues.

countries have difficulty in obtaining high tax revenues and therefore are characterized by less indebtedness than wealthy countries.

There are three state variables: consumption, capital and labor. Each of these variables depends on tax rates. Precisely changes of consumption over time are driven by all three tax rates; changes of capital depend on capital tax rate and labor tax rate and changes of labor are affected only by its own taxation. Differential equations for the state variables can be formalized as:

$$\frac{dc}{dt} = \left(a(1-\tau_c)-(1-a)\right)\left[(1-\tau_l)wl-\tau_k srk-b_t\right], \quad a \in [0.5,1], s \in [0,1] \tag{5}$$

Consumption is determined by disposable income (the expression in square brackets of equation (5)), proportion of taxed and untaxed consumption a and the level of the consumption tax rate τ_c. Disposable income comes from remuneration of labor less the money spent on capital taxes and bonds. Consumption is financed from labor income after labor taxation, payment of capital taxes and the purchase of bonds. We assume that capital income is not used for the financing of consumption. It should be stressed that now the bonds purchase plays the role of savings and there is no foreign income, contrary to the static models presented earlier. Obviously consumption tax (as well as two other tax rates) decreases the consumption growth in time.

$$\frac{dk}{dt} = (1-\tau_k)srk+(1-\tau_l)wl-c \tag{6}$$

Capital is created from capital income and labor income after tax payment of both production factors and expenses on gross consumption (implicit consumption and explicit consumption taxed with τ_c). The bonds affect capital formation only indirectly by the consumption. The government does not create capital in the economy, so the private formation of the capital is the only one.

$$\frac{dl}{dt} = nl-(1-\tau_l)wlh, \quad n,h>0 \tag{7}$$

The growth rate of labor in time is equal to the population growth rate n with a correction for the income effect induced by labor taxation. This effect is responsible for the increase of the labor offered by workers when the tax rate on labor is increasing. To modify the strength of this effect we add the parameter h, which is assumed to be positive to preserve the tax income effect but decreases its absolute value. Therefore the size of parameter h is a proxy of human capital accumulation and acts on the behalf of labor supply decrease in the long term. It should be noted that labor does not respond directly to the taxation of consumption or capital. Equations (5) and (7) unambiguously determine the level of labor and consumption tax in equilibrium because for known values of parameters taxes in equilibrium are unique. This is independent of the dynamic optimization procedure. Despite this, fixed taxation of labor and consumption has sizeable impact on the state variables in the equilibrium and this justifies their use in the model.

Taking the objective function and the differential equations for state variables, we can describe the dynamic maximization problem:

$$\max_{0\le\tau_c,\tau_k,\tau_w\le 1}\int_0^{\infty}\left(a\tau_c c+\tau_k sr\,k+\tau_l w l+b\right)e^{-\rho t}\,dt \tag{8}$$

where the constraints on the state variables are given by equations (5)-(7). ρ is the discount rate and should be considered as a positive number $\rho>0$. The value of discount rate protects the objective function to become infinite and allows obtaining internal solution of the system.

Necessary condition for the problem (8) under constrains (5)-(7) can be expressed using the current-value Hamiltonian function H. Let $\phi_1=nl-(1-\tau_l)wlh$, $\phi_2=(a(1-\tau_c)-(1-a))[(1-\tau_l)wl-\tau_k srk-b]$ and $\phi_3=(1-\tau_k)srk+(1-\tau_l)wl-c$ denote the right hand sides of the differential equations of state variables and μ_1, μ_2, μ_3 denote co-state variables associated with corresponding state variables. Then:

$$H=a\tau_c c+\tau_k srk+\tau_l wl+b+\mu_1\phi_1+\mu_2\phi_2+\mu_3\phi_3 \tag{9}$$

Firstly, the Maximum Principle calls for maximization of H due to the control variables. Current-value Hamiltonian is differentiable and nonlinear with respect control variables. Because we are looking for solutions which belong to the interior of the set of admissible controls (the optimum solution may also lie at the boundary of the control region) the following conditions have to be met:

$$\frac{\partial H}{\partial\tau_c}=ac+\frac{\partial b}{\partial\tau_c}+\sum_{i=1}^{3}\mu_i\frac{\partial\phi_i}{\partial\tau_c}=0 \tag{10}$$

$$\frac{\partial H}{\partial\tau_k}=sr\,k+\frac{\partial b}{\partial\tau_k}+\sum_{i=1}^{3}\mu_i\frac{\partial\phi_i}{\partial\tau_k}=0 \tag{11}$$

$$\frac{\partial H}{\partial\tau_l}=wl+\frac{\partial b}{\partial\tau_l}+\sum_{i=1}^{3}\mu_i\frac{\partial\phi_i}{\partial\tau_l}=0 \tag{12}$$

Equations (10)-(12) define co-state variables as functions of control and state variables. We solve them to get explicit formulas for co-state variables:

$$\mu_i=P_i\left(\tau_c,\tau_k,\tau_l,c,k,l\right),\quad i=1,2,3 \tag{13}$$

Secondly, the Maximum Principle gives us equations of motion for the co-state variables, which look as follows:

$$\dot{\mu}_1 = -\frac{\partial H}{\partial c} + \rho\mu_1 \tag{14}$$

$$\dot{\mu}_2 = -\frac{\partial H}{\partial l} + \rho\mu_2 \tag{15}$$

$$\dot{\mu}_3 = -\frac{\partial H}{\partial k} + \rho\mu_3 \tag{16}$$

Thirdly, we derive equations of motion of the control variables. To do it we substitute formulas (13) and their derivatives with respect to time to the equations of motion of co-state variables (14)-(16). We obtain differential equations which describe dynamics of the control variables (τ_c, τ_k, τ_l), in the implicit form:

$$Q_i\left(\tau_c, \tau_k, \tau_l, c, k, l, \dot{\tau}_c, \dot{\tau}_k, \dot{\tau}_l\right) = 0, \quad i = 1,2,3 \tag{17}$$

And fourthly, we combine equations of motion of the state variables with derived equations of motion of the control variables to get dynamic system whose equilibrium represents long-run optimal tax rates and long-run optimal levels of capital, labor and consumption.

Finally, we should find the solutions of six-dimensional system of nonlinear differential equations representing the dynamics of state and control variables (equations (5)-(7) and three equations derived according to (17)). Unfortunately, this problem cannot be solved analytically, so we need to find equilibrium tax rates and equilibrium levels of the state variables numerically.

3. The numerical analysis

We need to run a numerical simulation to discover some features of the obtained solution because described model cannot be solved analytically. Especially the value of parameters used in numerical simulation should help to describe the behavior of the three control variables, the level of bond issues and state variables. As the most interesting parameters we found the behavior of: *a*, *s*, *r* and *p* because they represent the shadow and explicit consumption, capital income tax avoidance, return on capital and the market tolerance for debt. The first two of them refer to the tax competition and possibilities of taxation different tax bases. The third is connected with the capital accumulation and the last captures the attitudes to the fiscal solvency. For that reason the four scenarios can be investigated when other parameters are set fixed.

The values of other parameters in the simulation are determined in the following way. The exogenous growth rate of population is set at 2%, so $n = 0.05$, the discount rate $\rho = 0.1$, the wage w $= 0.005$ and the parameter of human capital formation $h = 7$. These values are invariant for all simulations. We assume that explicit consumption should be higher than implicit one, so the parameter a cannot be lower than 0.5 and higher than 1. This means that more than half of the total consumption is taxed and in this case taxation of whole consumption is possible. This condition eliminates the taxation of consumption from outside the range 0-1.

The first scenario examines the impact of the parameter a (the explicit rate of consumption). Setting parameters for numerical simulation at levels: $s = 0.7$; $r = 0.15$; $w = 0.005$; $\rho = 0.1$; $n = 0.02$; $h = 7$; $p = 3$ one can present the value of tax rates and bonds in the equilibrium as a function of explicit consumption a value. Looking at Fig. 1 one can see that taxation of capital in equilibrium is growing with the parameter a but at different rates, for a low a – with decreasing dynamic and for high a – with increasing dynamic. The taxation of consumption is also increasing with the share of explicit consumption but the speed of this adjustment is roughly constant. Higher taxations involve higher bond issuance because the credibility of government is increasing. This is true despite the labor taxation remains constant.

Unfortunately, obtained results indicate that if the level of hidden consumption is high then neither of tax instruments can improve the budgetary situation of a government. Saying differently, the government should ensure that the consumption will not escape taxation if the fiscal solvency requirement is to be met. This is very important conclusion in the context of fiscal solvency. The consumption in the equilibrium at first increases and then decreases as the a becomes larger. There is apparent maximum of consumption for the share of explicit consumption equal about 85%. Probably the increasing dynamics of capital tax is responsible for the drop of consumption. This result is particularly interesting if the government is going to curb the shadow economy without harming consumption. For this level of explicit consumption the corresponding tax rate on capital reaches about 25%. Despite the rising taxation, the capital level in equilibrium is growing together with explicit consumption share. The same is true for labor but the labor taxation is not a causative factor in this case because it stays constant).

Figure 23: *Equilibrium tax rates as function of explicit consumption share.*

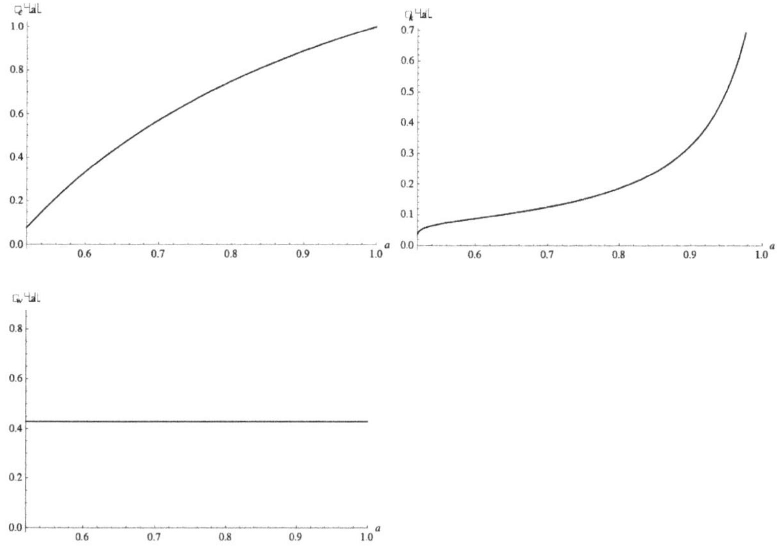

Source: Calculation in Mathematica 9.

Figure 24: *Equilibrium volume of consumption, capital and labor as a function of explicit consumption share.*

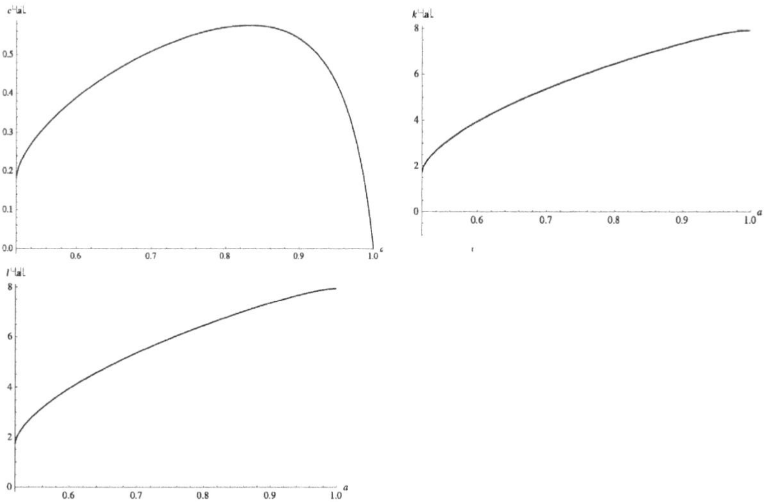

Source: Calculation in Mathematica 9.

The bonds issuance is increasing with explicit consumption share. It should be noticed that the value of bonds is about to double with the increase of explicit consumption from 0.5 to 1. Bonds issuance cannot be perceived as a remedy for the inability of tax revenue collection. This issue is most likely induced by the necessity of fiscal solvency rule to be met. The government can borrow more when the share of implicit consumption is high but in this situation the other tax revenues are scarce and the investors are not willing to buy many bonds.

Figure 25: *Equilibrium volume of bonds as a function of explicit consumption share.*

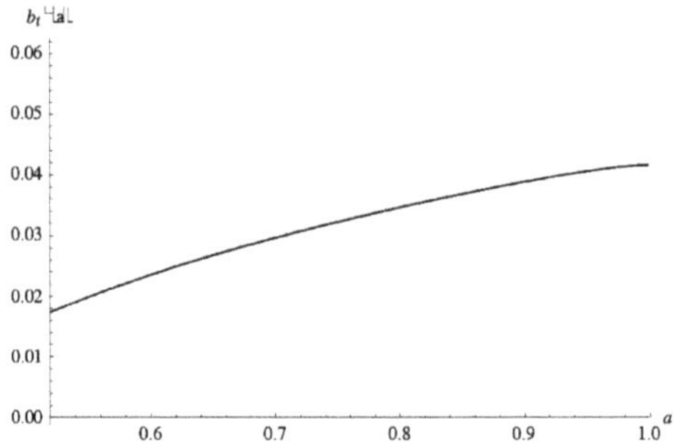

Source: Calculation in Mathematica 9.

The second scenario describes the impact of parameter *s*, referring to the shifting (or hiding) of capital income. The parameters loaded to simulation are: $r=0.15$; $w=0.005$; $\rho=0.1$; $n=0.02$; $h=7$; $p=3$; $a=0.9$. Now the explicit consumption is set at relatively high level (only 10% of consumption is hidden) and the parameter *s* is variable. As one can recall high *s* means low capital income shifting. The most pronounced effect links to the capital income taxation, which is strongly decreasing with the increase of *s*. This differs significantly from the reaction of consumption tax and labor tax which stay constant. The two tax rates seem to be independent of the capital income shifting activity of taxpayers. The level of debt is growing because labor tax revenue increases due to the substitution of capital with labor. The capital accumulation in the country tends to be lower which affects the productivity and deteriorates consumption. In this situation government prefers bond financing and constant taxation of consumption and labor. This is an interesting result because on the one side it advocates for the high taxation of capital when capital in the country is abundant irrespectively of the income-shifting possibilities. On the other side, high *s* provides the low level of capital, so the high shifting possibilities are beneficial for the capital accumulation while the low one are destructive. If we would like to concentrate on the high consumption we should stimulate higher shifting possibilities, for example promoting openness of the economy and abandon all restriction imposed on international capital movements.

Figure 26: *Equilibrium tax rates as function of capital tax shifting parameter.*

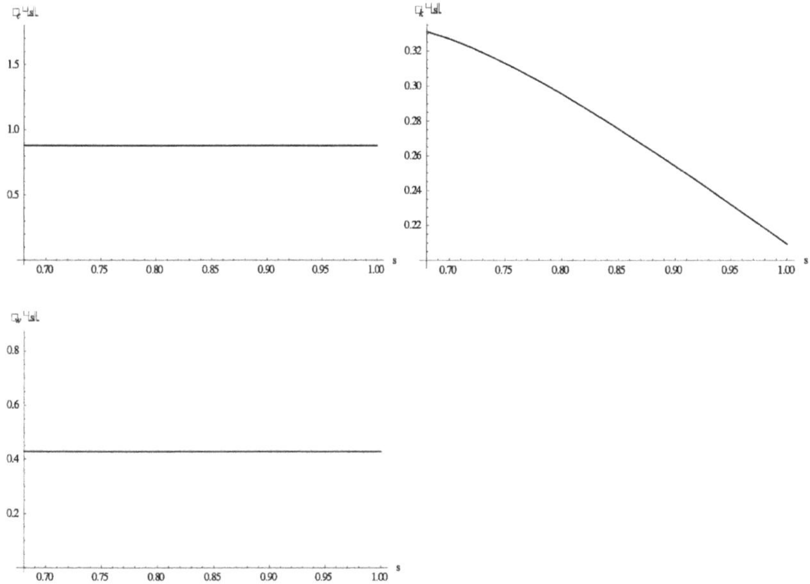

Source: Calculation in Mathematica 9.

Figure 27: *Equilibrium volume of: consumption, capital and labor as a function of capital tax shifting parameter.*

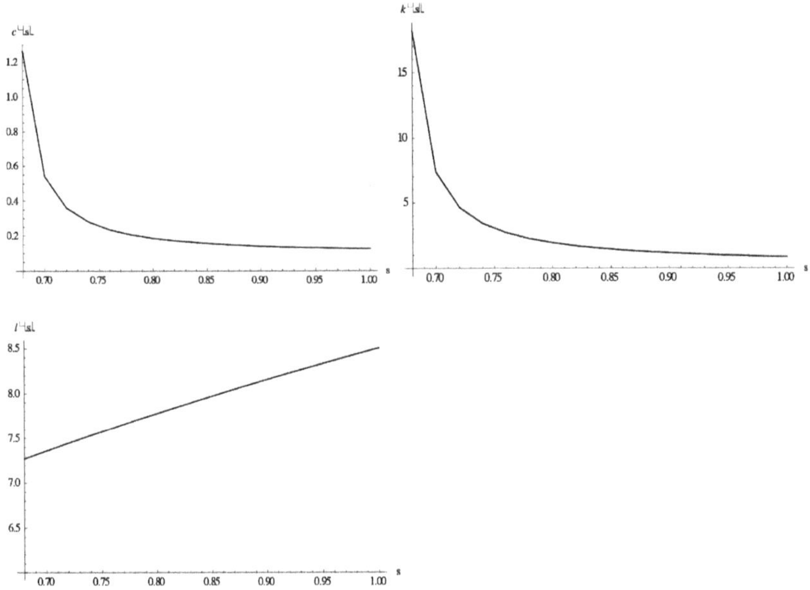

Source: Calculation in Mathematica 9.

Figure 28: *Equilibrium volume of bonds as a function of capital tax shifting parameter.*

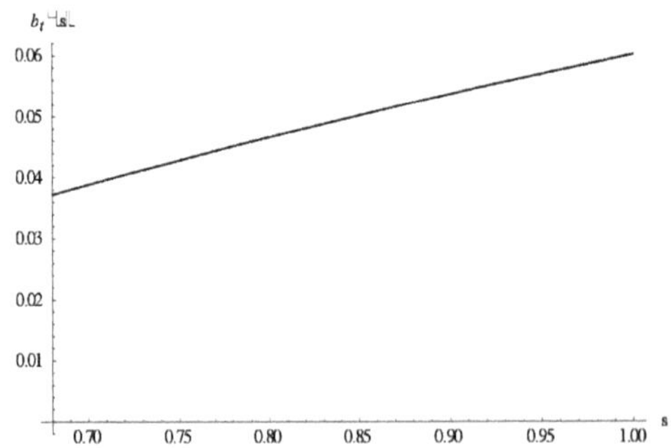

Source: Calculation in Mathematica 9.

The third scenario describes the impact the level of interest income (return) on capital – identified with parameter r. The simulation involves the following values of parameters: $s=0.8$; $w=0.005$; $\rho=0.1$; $n=0.02$; $h=7$; $p=3$; $a=0.9$. The result referring to tax rates resembles the changes of the increase of capital tax shifting parameter. Tax rates on consumption and labor turn out to be unaffected while the taxation of capital follows decreasing trend. The capital and consumption decline and the labor replace capital. Despite the lower consumption and capital accumulation, debt financing can be higher (the issuance of bonds is higher) because taxation of labor compensates the loss of other tax revenues. The results are predictable, because higher return on capital is typical for low capital accumulation and the latter decreases the labor productivity inducing the intensification of labor involvement. However this type of equilibrium is not preferred by governments.

Figure 29: *Equilibrium tax rates as a function of return on capital.*

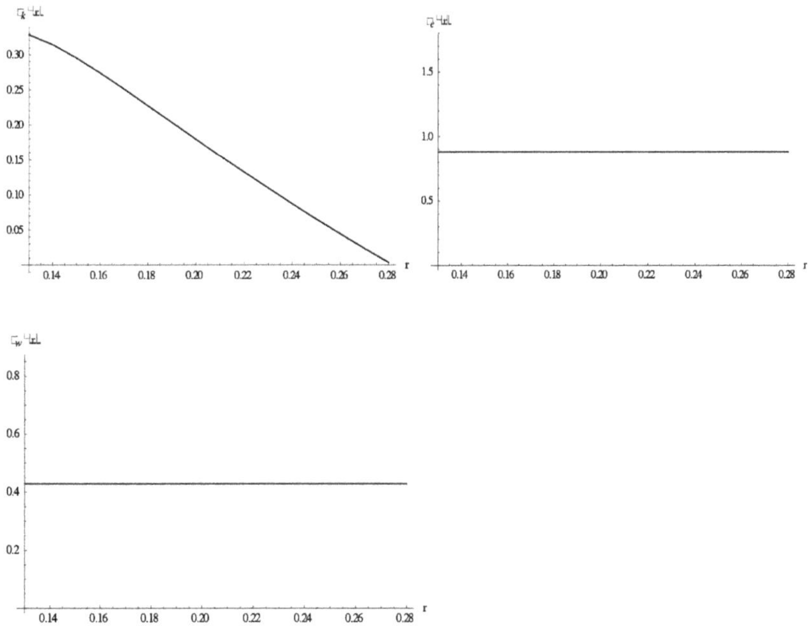

Source: Calculation in Mathematica 9.

Figure 30: *Equilibrium volume of capital and consumption as a function of return on capital.*

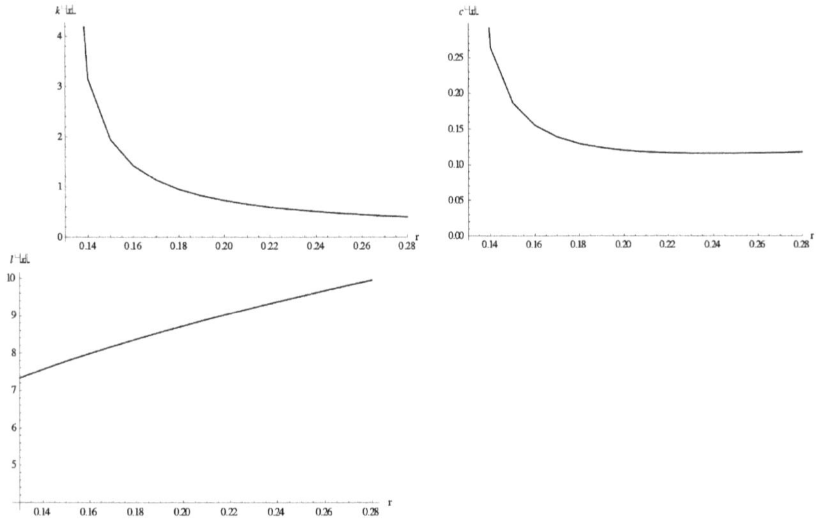

Source: Calculation in Mathematica 9.

Figure 31: *Equilibrium volume of bonds as function of return on capital.*

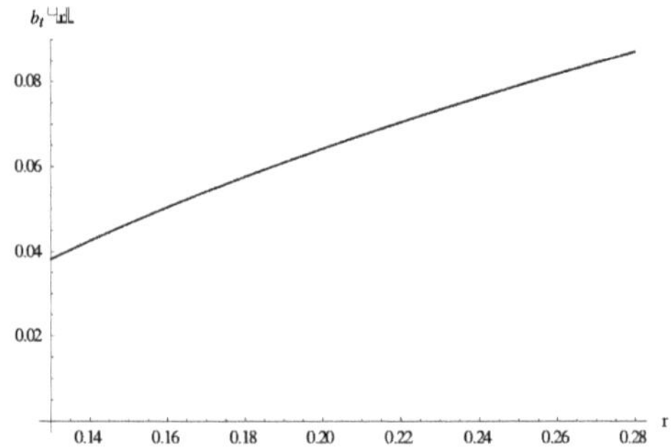

Source: Calculation in Mathematica 9.

The fourth scenario examines the impact of parameter p – the tolerance for debt or more precisely the reaction of financial market for the relation of debt to the proxy of production. The parameters used here take the values: $s=0.8$; $r=0.15$; $w=0.005$; $\rho=0.1$; $n=0.02$; $h=7$; $a=0.9$. This scenario is especially interesting because it stimulates an increase of capital, labor and consumption without tax rates modification. In fact all three taxes remain unaffected when tolerance is “growing” but the tax revenues are higher because of the increasing tax bases. The increasing tolerance for debt forces the outburst of debt. As a consequence higher debt subsidizes for tax rates increase. The capital, labor and consumption are all growing and this fosters further bonds increase. But arguing reversely, decreasing tolerance for debt should not be compensated by the tax increase. Probably this pinpoints the independence of tax and debt policy in the long term. The most astonishing result should be the assertion that the best reply for the disturbances on the financial market is simply to do nothing with tax burden. This scenario explains either why the governments are interested in the debt financing instead of the tax adjustment. As one can see the tax adjustment for the credibility problem is futile and cannot impact the resentment prevailing on the financial market.

Figure 32: *Equilibrium tax rates as a function of debt tolerance parameter.*

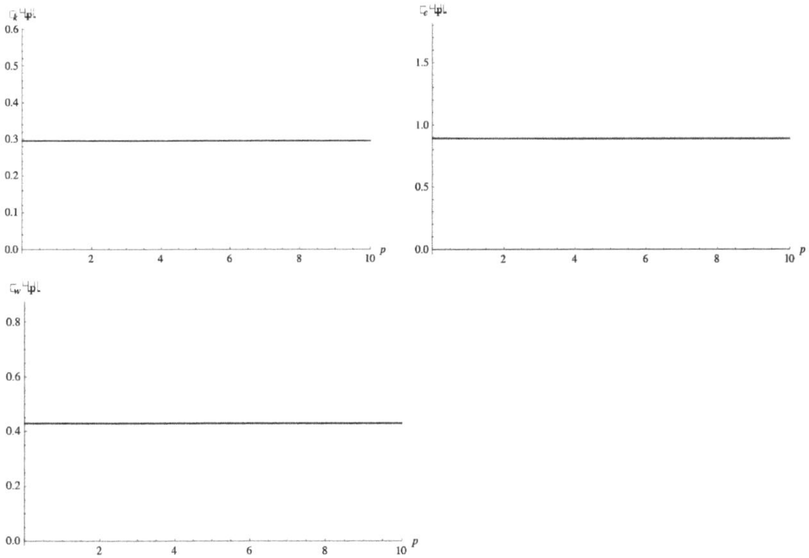

Source: Calculation in Mathematica 9.

Figure 33: *Equilibrium volume of capital, consumption and labor as a function of debt tolerance parameter.*

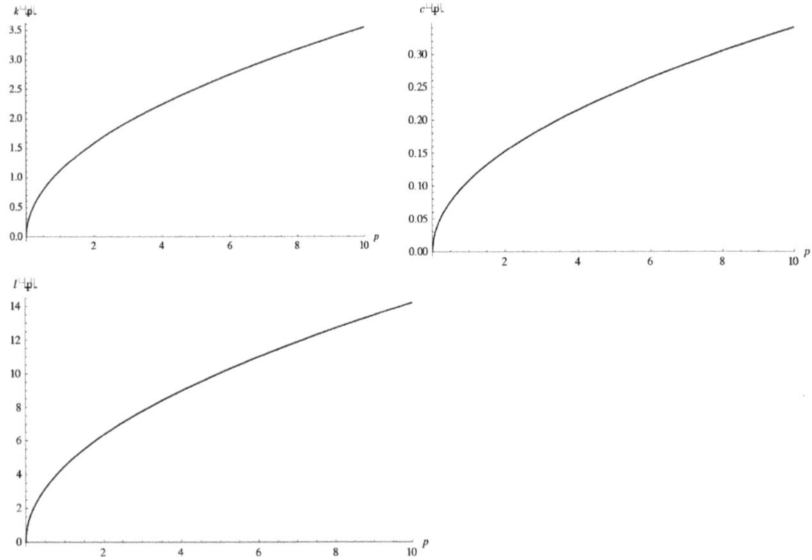

Source: Calculation in Mathematica 9.

Figure 34: *Equilibrium volume of bonds as a function of debt tolerance parameter.*

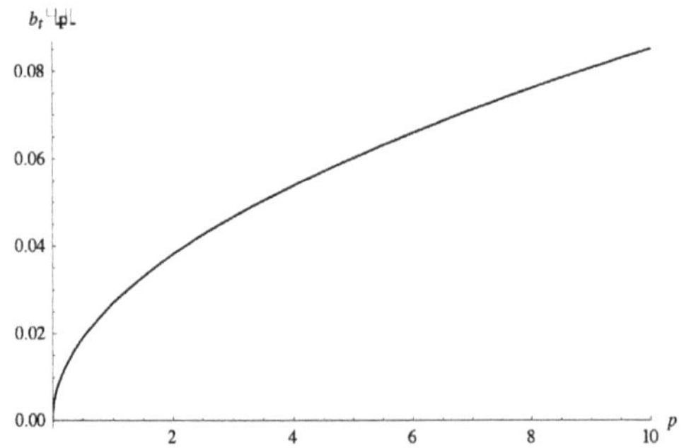

Source: Calculation in Mathematica 9.

Summarizing the dynamic model the three different patterns are observed. In the first the increasing explicit consumption stimulates higher taxation on consumption and capital together with the increasing value of bonds. In the second the low shifting activity (high s) or high rate of return (r) decreases the taxation of capital but has no impact on other tax rates. In this case, capital is replaced with labor; the consumption diminishes as well as accumulated capital. The characterized changes do not interfere with debt financing, which grows intensively spurred by revenue collected from labor taxation. The third pattern involves greater acceptance for the debt and provides an increase of tax bases and amount of debt but without changes in tax rates.

Chapter 4
Spatial modeling of fiscal policy and debt

1. Introduction

European Union regulations as well as country level regulations, set the fiscal policy as the independent one, anchored in countries' local conditions. As proved by theoretical models and literature review, fiscal policy is strongly related to the financial situation of governments. The debt changes as well as other variations of macroeconomic parameters should cause tax rates adjustments and subsequently should affect the budgetary revenues. However, in open economies most of macroeconomic parameters are interdependent between countries, because of trade relations and cross-border trade, the mobility of production factors, flows of goods, services, people and capital, common currency, interest and exchange rates differentials, historical or institutional factors etc. Thus even if fiscal policy is nominally independent then effects of fiscal policy do not impact only a given country but also the interconnected economies. There appears so called spillover effect which can be perceived as the broader interdependence occurring between fiscal parameters in different countries. Precisely the spatial spillovers effect is understood as an impact of government policy in one country on performance of other neighboring economies, with regard to the distance in space between them. Contrary to the predictions of tax (or fiscal) competition hypotheses these relations cover all intended (or direct) actions of the government but also any unintended (or indirect) changes of fiscal variables. Both elements taken together determine the total impact of fiscal policies on sovereign debt in open economies. Considering the reaction on the changes of debt, obviously one can expect the rise in tax rates as the simplest mechanisms of financing financial gap between revenues and spending of governments. However, the complexity of the impact of tax rate changes stimulates the needs for fiscal policy real fine-tuning, which is necessary not to overshoot the objective or uselessly not to disturb the economy. This is especially important because according to dynamic model result, the tax rate adjustments in the long term are superfluous. An increase of tax rates as a reaction on the increasing debt needs can be ineffective in many cases (providing less revenues to a budget) and not feasible (impossible to introduce) for example for political reasons. Therefore it would be interesting to investigate whether changes which occurred in the last decade in the European Union countries are consistent with theoretical predictions sketched in previous chapters.

One of the methods, for proving or denying the hypotheses about tax rates behavior, is to perform an econometric analysis on a macroeconomic data. Unfortunately the econometric analysis of debt and tax rates interrelations for European countries is not straightforward. This is caused by several political and economic reasons altering the fiscal policies of European governments in the last decade. Recently European countries were under great structural changes, starting from the introduction of common currency euro in 2002, through the significant European Union enlargement in 2004, accepting the new financial perspective in 2007 to financial crisis starting in 2008. All those events can be treated as mile stones of the changes in the European continent. However, some government actions had opposite effects, which throughout the channels of spatial spillover could easily blur the pattern of fiscal policy adaptation. It cannot also be excluded that some of the tax adjustments could partially offset each other in different periods. For example, taxes on labor can be lowered at first to prevent the outburst of unemployment and after that raised to decrease the budgetary deficit and regain the credibility of financial market. Unfortunately, it can look like as inconsistent fiscal policy, because in one period the labor taxation can increase with the debt and in the other – decrease. Probably the most observed fiscal adjustments do not reflect an independent government's policies but rather they are the compositions of well-coordinated and also uncoordinated institutional and economic actions. Sometimes this action is a consequence of economic integration, sometimes it is triggered by tax competition forces, imitation of neighboring policies or uneven impact of financial crisis spillover affecting selected countries in different times and to different degree.

This diversity of interactions increases the importance of an econometric modeling which takes into account not only the relationships between countries (captured well in panel data analysis) – but also the neighborhood relationships occurring in space. It should be expected that the impact exerted by the various fiscal policies have limited spatial and temporal coverage. Second expectation is that policy pursued by neighbors has stronger impact than policy performed by other, more distant countries. For this reason it was decided to use spatial econometrics methods for reciprocal impact of tax rates and debt and spillover effects between variables. The spatial econometrics model includes the tax competition or tax-imitation-policy on the one hand, together with fiscal situation of individual countries on the other hand. This approach is suitable to distinguish between general spillover effect and the effects induced by internal factors like those generated by national macroeconomic variables. Through skillful selection of weights measuring the effects of spatial separation it is also possible to discriminate between short- and long-distance interactions and time-specific variation. This spatio-temporal aspect of inter-country policy coordination seems to be underdeveloped in recent literature. Till now there are few studies showing the spatial patterns of fiscal policy dynamics from the statistical point of view. The existing econometric studies also hardly use spatial methodology to capture spatial interactions resulting from the fiscal decisions of neighboring and other countries[21]. Last but not least, the spatial econometrics can help to check the accuracy of postulates formulated by New Economic Geography. It refers mainly to the impact of distance as a proxy of increasing transaction costs.

The crucial point of this chapter is to analyze spatio-temporal patterns of tax policy changes of the last decade in Europe and to assess the interactions with governments' debts. We decided to cover the whole decade to avoid the determination of results by the crisis adjustments only and to extend the range of data. The latter is especially important in the study of so many countries with spatial and time dependencies requiring the use of lags. The study strives to answer two specified important questions in the context of debt explanation:

1) Are the fiscal policy changes inter-related between countries? Are the fiscal policy changes inter-related over time?
2) Is there any spatial spillover effect in transmission of tax rate changes to other countries?

These questions will be answered on the basis of the analysis of European countries data. It should be noted that this analysis requires reversing the relationship between debt and taxes. We would like to use one equation with several fiscal tools instead of three equations for each tax rates (on capital, labor and consumption). Therefore we estimate one equation of debt explained by three tax rates and the set of other macroeconomic variables. Obviously this relation can be estimated in different ways. The differences include: the two forms of spatial weights matrix

21 Literature taking into account the spatial aspect in studies on debt and taxes is narrow. Romero and Burkey (2011) use panel spatial methods and argue that spatial effects are very strong in relation to the EU economies and the impact of debt on GDP growth. Baldacci, Dell'Erba and Poghosyan (2011) show that there is a clear spillover in the valuation of the bond market, which is present in both the developed and developing economies, and results from its spatial proximity and financial and trade linkages. Bordignon *et al.* (2003) conducted a spatial analysis of the local tax rates for Italy and Brueckner (2003) presented a spatial analysis of local taxation and local government spending.

better seizing the closer or more removed interactions between countries, fixed, random or pooled panel effects and the use of so called OLS a-spatial model as a reference version of the econometric model. The last model does not include panel effects and spatial matrix weights and therefore can be used as a benchmark. However, econometric modeling is not the first step. To fully understand patterns of changes in debt and tax rates in the European countries over last decade we run detailed spatio-temporal statistical analysis of data. Multivariate plots and Moran plots will be applied. All this quantitative analyses are designed to answer the questions set above.

2. The measurement of debt and tax changes

Finding spillover effect in invisible flows like effects of fiscal policy is not a trivial task. It should be noted that fiscal policy does not provide tangible trans-border effects like for example capital or trade flows. With traditional time-series econometrics, one can easily find relations in time, modeling time lags of reactions and controlling for general trends stemming from economic fluctuations. In fact, this is one-dimensional analysis neglecting the relations in space. When starting spatial or better spatio-temporal research, we add second dimension of the analytics, as we are going to observe changes over time with regard to their location and spatial impact.

The general approach to the spatial econometric modeling consists of two stages. In the first, one should recognize the time pattern and in the second observe the spatial reactions. Following this idea, the statistics of variables over time are calculated and presented in the multivariate plot (Peng, 2008). The graph (Figure 35) presents sovereign debt changes occurring in 34 investigated countries. It should be read as follows: each country changes are reproduced by the gray scale, from low values (light gray) to the high (dark gray). Light colors of two countries are poorly comparable in the value, but well comparable in the relative level. For example, in given period when two countries have a light color, both of them have relatively low indebtedness, taking into account their whole history of sovereign debt level in considered period. Chart allows for the assessment of variability over time, with only weak inter-comparisons during the period. The relative level of debt in the country is presented in the panel to the right of the main panel with gray colors. The average level of debt in the country means that the relative debt is zero, values on the left of these points represent lower level of debt and values on the right higher ones. Panels below multivariate charts reflect general average of variable. In this case this is relative change to the average level of the debt in considered period.

Figure 35: *Multivariate plot for sovereign debt.*

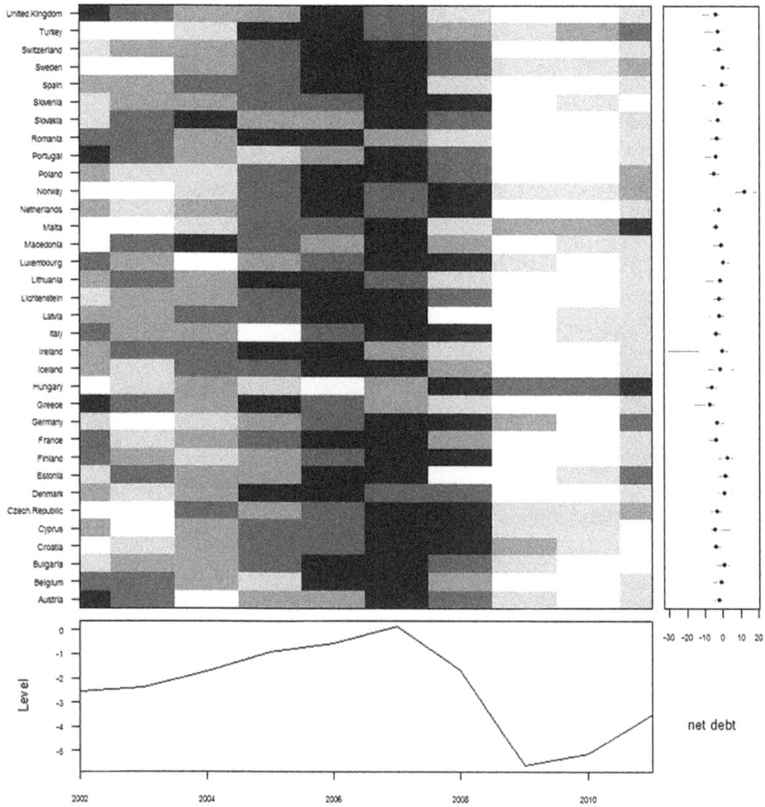

Source: Own analysis on data from IMF

The similar calculation can be applied to other variables, especially to the behavior of tax rates which are of special interest in the context of the book. The juxtaposition of tax rates changes is presented as Figures 36, 37 and 38. These figures refer respectively to the: capital, labor and consumption taxes calculated as implied tax rates for the same set of 34 countries. Implied tax rates are the product of changes involving nominal tax rates as well as tax bases. Some of the changes are determined by the legislature and some are the effect of action undertaken by taxpayers (deliberate or accidental). For example it can refer to the tax planning, tax avoidance strategies or to the changes of business activity in the economic cycle.

Figure 36: *Multivariate plot on individual tax rates on capital.*

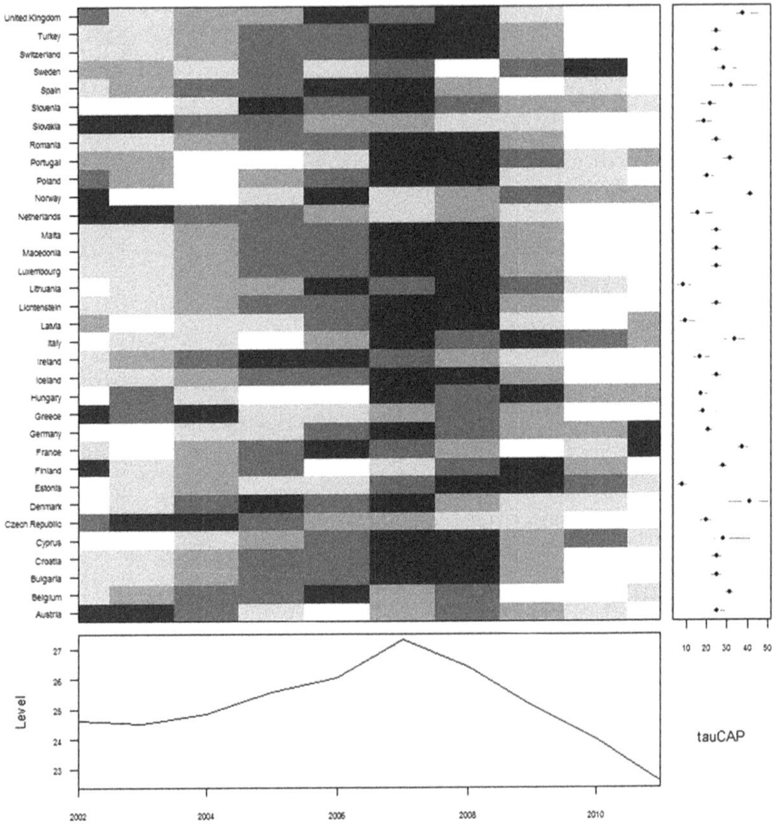

Source: Own analysis on data from EUROSTAT

From multivariate plot of capital tax (Figure 36) one can see that most countries decided to raise capital taxation in the 2007, in the year before the financial crisis affected most of the European countries. However there were several countries which have increased taxes before this date. It refers to the following countries: Spain, Norway, France and Belgium. United Kingdom, Slovenia and Lithuania have done slight movements up and down, probably trying to investigate the reaction of financial markets and the economy but without clear direction of adjustment. The last group of countries: Slovakia, Netherlands, Greece, Czech Republic and Austria, consequently encouraged the capital inflow by lowering tax rates in a constant manner.

Figure 37: *Multivariate plot on individual tax rates on labor.*

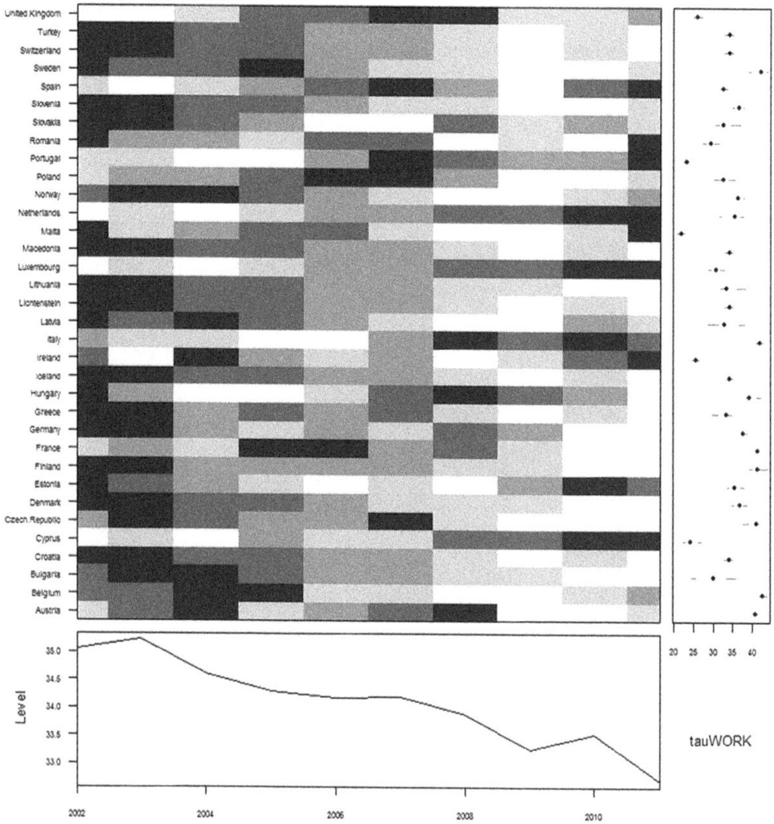

Source: Own analysis on data from EUROSTAT

The changes of labor taxation reveal different pattern of changes (Figure 37). The most of countries reached their minimum tax rate on labor in 2009. Declining trend of labor tax was evidenced for: Turkey, Switzerland, Sweden, Slovenia, Norway, Malta, Lithuania, Lichtenstein, Latvia, Iceland, Finland, Denmark, Croatia and Bulgaria. No strictly declining pattern exhibited: United Kingdom, Spain, Slovakia, Romania, Poland, Hungary, Estonia, Czech Republic, Austria, France and Germany. Tax rate on labor increased in: Portugal, Netherlands, Luxemburg, Italy, Ireland, Estonia and Cyprus. However the general tendency of labor taxation in Europe is evidently declining over time. This tendency has been accelerated after 2007. This can hint the increasing concern about the unemployment after the possible increase of labor tax burden for solvency reason.

Figure 38: *Multivariate plot of tax rate on consumption.*

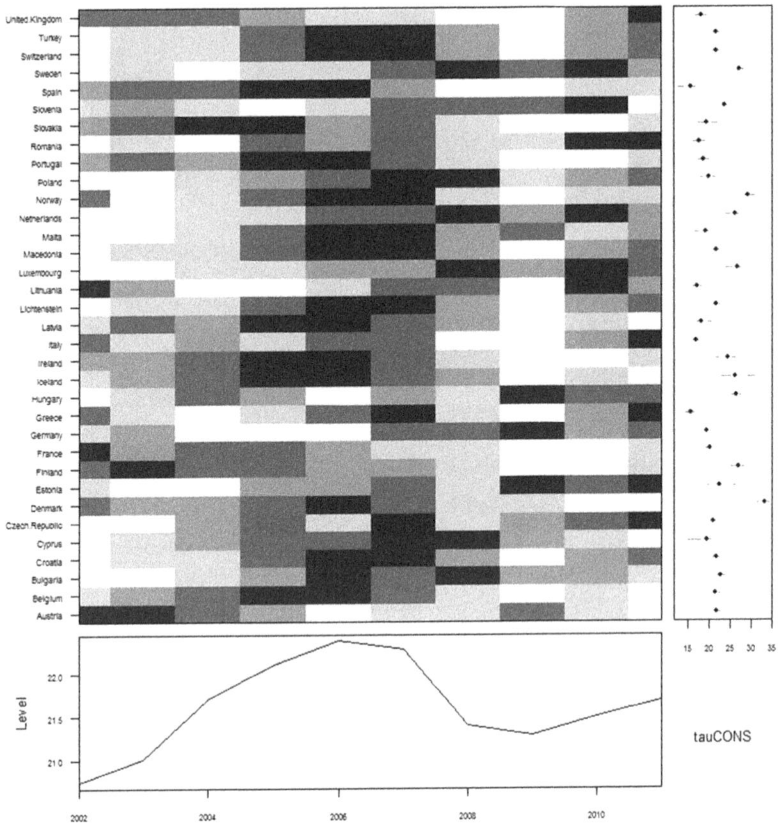

Source: Own analysis on data from EUROSTAT

The last graph (Figure 38) presents the changes of consumption tax in the consecutive years (2002-2011). One can see that tax rates on consumption reached their peak shortly before the beginning of the crisis, particularly in years 2005-2007. In 2005 these concerned: Spain, Portugal, Latvia, Ireland, Iceland and Belgium, in 2006: Bulgaria, Croatia, Denmark, Italy, Lichtenstein, Malta, Macedonia, Norway, Switzerland and Turkey and in 2007: Poland, Lithuania, Greece, Germany, Estonia, Czech Republic and Cyprus. However, there were some countries which decided to introduce anti-cyclical policy with declining consumption tax rates in the whole period. For example, it was the case of Hungary and Austria. These two countries noted minimum of their tax rate on consumption in 2006. It should be noted that a time coincidence of tax on consumption with the debt is also visible but beyond the commented graph.

The dynamics of relation occurring in space can be analyzed with spatial statistics instruments. Prevalent statistical measure of global spatial autocorrelation is Moran's I. It is spatial measure of autocorrelation under assumed spatial pattern of neighborhood provided with spatial weights matrix. Indicators of spatial associations measure the difference between analyzed region and its neighbors. When similar values are located in neighboring regions then it is perceived as positive spatial autocorrelation. Extreme positive spatial autocorrelation, when there are two clubs of values only (high and low), is regarded as spatial heterogeneity. It evaluates processes and patterns that appear throughout the territory. The value of this spatial statistics depends on the difference between the test and the average value. The test is based on the covariance matrix, similarly to the Pearson test in correlation of variables. For values of Moran's I between $-1 < I < 0$ the negative correlation is observed, which means that similar values touch each other less often than random. For values between $0 < I < 1$ positive correlation is observed, which means that similar values touch each other more often than random. However because this relation has been shown in the Introduction to the book (in the form of Moran's I scatterplots), therefore it is omitted here. It should be only mentioned that the space coincidence generally confirms time conjuncture in tax rates adjustment. This especially applies to the 2005 and 2007. It confirms that tax rate changes in neighboring countries were relatively similar in these years in size and direction.

Finally to find detailed coefficients of relations between explained phenomena and exogenous information, including spatial spillovers effects, spatial econometric techniques can be applied. The most advanced way of detecting spatial patterns is to run spatial econometric methods, which include spatial relations as component of error autocorrelation and spatial lag of dependent variable. Spatial lags are understood as the weighted average from neighboring locations. Beyond spatial lag, spatio-temporal lags can be used, which are then weighted average from neighboring locations from previous period. With correctly specified equation, one can easily filter out common relations and observe spatial effects over time.

Additionally, direct and indirect impacts can be calculated to interpret strength of changes in the same region/country and in the neighborhood. They are applied in models with spatial lag of dependent variable, because simultaneity of phenomena on both sides of equation sharply limits the possibility of reasonable interpretation and forecasting. Thus, for final model, impacts are calculated and used in explanation of the results of spatial econometric models instead of traditional betas. According to LeSage & Pace (2009), the direct impact is viewed as an impact of change of x in i location on change of y in i location. The indirect effect is an impact of change of x in i location on change of y in j location ($i \neq j$) and is interpreted as a spillover effect. The direct impact is given as the total sum of diagonal elements of the partial derivatives matrix $Sr(W)$, calculated for a given variable. The total impact is the sum of all elements of this matrix. The indirect impact is the difference between the two. Thus, in the spatial panel models with spatial lags, the betas are only an intermediate step necessary to select the best model but the final interpretation of explanatory variables should be done on impacts.

3. Dataset

The study uses a panel data for $T = 10$ years (2002-2011), and $N = 34$ European countries, which allows for a spatial panel estimation method to be applied. This panel is not balanced due to the lack of some data in non-OECD and European Union countries. Many authors prefers to remove such observations in order to obtain a balanced panel (e.g. Claeys *et al.*, 2012), but this leads to a loss of neighbor ties and significantly disturbs the spatial weights matrix. Due to the utmost care for possible best representation of neighbor relations, we have used the method of multiple imputation of missing values. As Honaker & King (2010) show, this approach does not significantly impair the average estimates of the parameters but facilitates the modeling of neighbor relations.

To explain the public debt in the model, the main tax variables (tax rates on consumption, capital and labor) and macroeconomic variables (the GDP growth rate, the unemployment rate, and – in relation to GDP – exports, imports, gross debt, domestic demand, net debt, investment and savings) have been used. The public debt is determined by many endogenous and exogenous factors. The former include government's fiscal credibility determined by current borrowing levels and the amount of outstanding public debt. The latter are current economic situation determined by market concentration, interbank interest rates and many other factors. Therefore the following variables referring to financial markets were applied: the Herfindhal index (*Herfindahl*) for bank loan market monopolization, the share of domestic ownership of capital (*alpha*), the government bond yields (*Bondrate*), and the investment position (*netLEND_BORROW2gdp*).

The data were collected from Eurostat, ECB and IMF. From the EUROSTAT database the following data were obtained: the tax rates on consumption (*tauCON*), capital (*tauCAP*) and labor (*tauLABOR*) as the implied tax rates[22], the interest rate of bonds (*Bondrate*) as the price of 10-year government bonds, domestic demand calculated in PPS as a share of GDP (*domdem2gdp*), exports and imports as a share of GDP (*export2gdp*, *import2gdp*), the annual growth rate of GDP (*gdp_growth_rate*). We believe that implied tax rates are the best proxies of the actual tax burden. From the ECB database we have obtained the share of residents – owners of capital (*alpha*) which was calculated as the share of domestic ownership of capital relative to the sum of domestic and foreign capital, the degree of monopoly in the capital market (*Herfindahl*), the dummy variable that specifies the membership in the euro area (*euroZONE*), investment position (*INVESTpos*) calculated as the financial investment relative to GDP, the savings relative to disposable income (*savings2income*). From the IMF database we derived the unemployment rate (*unemployment*), the investment relative to GDP (*invest2gdp*), gross state budget deficit relative to GDP (*grossdebt2gdp*) and government net loans relative to GDP (*netLEND_BORROW2gdp*).

To check for the possible multicolinearity, the Pearson correlations have been applied. The Pearson correlation are on the graph of Moran's I type (Figure 39)[23]. The correlations refer to the variables used in the spatial econometric analysis. Smaller circles represent weaker spatial interdependence and gray tints provide the information about the strength and direction of the interrelation. Negative values, according to the scale, are in pale grey-color and positive values in the dark one. The smallest circles provide coefficients close to 0. The insignificant correlations at $\alpha = 0.05$ level are marked with crosses. The correlation is the highest between the same variables (which means the largest circles) on the diagonal. The relation is strictly positive and equal one, so the color of circles on the diagonal is black.

22 For the details of calculating implied tax rates refer to EUROSTAT's *Taxation Trends in Europe* (2014).

23 See the comment of this type of graph included in the Introduction chapter.

Figure 39: *Pearson correlation between variables.*

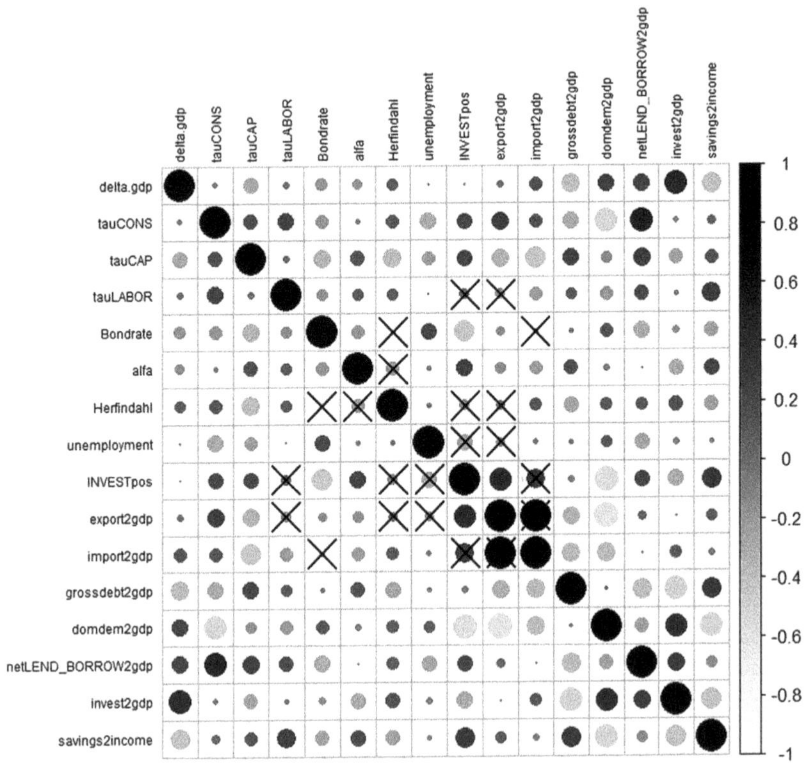

Source: Own analysis on data from EUROSTAT, IMF, OECD, ECB

Variables of interest (tauCONS, tauCAP, tauLABOR) are selectively correlated. Strong, significant and positive correlation appears between all tax rates and net lending and borrowing, what is natural consequence of budget stability. Positive correlation unexpectedly appears between savings and taxation. Higher taxation, should decrease disposable income and then reduce private savings. However in affluent societies, the higher savings are reasonable because of higher standard of living and lower share of necessities in private budgets despite the higher taxation financing expanded state functions. A very high positive correlation exhibits exports and imports in relation to GDP, which means that countries symmetrically engage in international trade. The high negative correlation can be observed between exports and domestic demand in relation to GDP ratio. The relationship between domestic demand and imports is also negative but weaker.

4. Spatial modeling of debt determinants

We expect consumers, producers and government to adapt to the tax rates changes in the short term. This is because current fiscal policy responds explicitly or implicitly to an economic cycle and to the fiscal condition of a government. For example government can increase tax rates in response to the increase of debt or the tax bases can be altered because of the economic or regulatory reasons. Therefore the concentration on short-term relation between net debt changes and tax rates seems to be justified. It should be noted that mutual reactions of tax policy and debt are well-known from other studies. For example there exists feedback loop in which causality of debt and taxation is researched well. Following Egert (2012), fiscal policy reactions are non-linear and dependent on country's situation. For higher-debt countries pro-cyclical reactions were found, neutral in averaged-debt countries and counter-cyclical in high debt countries.

Reading the literature on spatial static panel models, long term relations are usually modeled with "between" estimators, while for short-term effects the "within" estimators are applied in the Fixed Effects model. Random Effects models are obtained as the weighted average of "within" and "between" estimators (e.g. Kuh, 1959; Houthakker, 1965). Between estimators require applying the time/group averages of data. As a consequence it makes the intra-group variability smooth.

However, the purpose of the econometric modeling is to find instant reaction of debt on fiscal policy or economic changes. Therefore we decided to build the model in a manner explaining one-year changes of net debt with one-year tax rates changes, controlling for the macroeconomic, institutional and financial situation. This specification, despite the concentration on the short-term adjustments, includes also the long-term perspective because the panel covers ten years of data. In the panel estimation these short-term reactions are averaged over long-term period. It allows for long-term assessment of the process, the stability and relevance of the revealed dependencies. The tool for this is the use of a spatial autoregressive model with spatial lag of dependent variable Wy and/or spatio-temporal lag of y. The latter controls for local clustering over space and reflects the inter-neighborhood relations. Spatial coefficients at spatial lag of y and spatial autocorrelation of error term cover spatial spillovers effects.

Precisely, the form of the econometric model is given as:

$$y_{it} = \lambda Wy_{it} + \beta X_{it} + \upsilon_i + \tau_t + u_{it} \tag{1}$$

where W is the spatial weights matrix based on criteria of defined neighboring countries, υ_i are individual effects for particular countries, τ_t are time effects for consecutive years, u_{it} are the spatial errors. The latter should meet the following condition:

$$u_{it} = f(Wu, \mu) + \varepsilon_{it} \tag{2}$$

where Wu is the autocorrelated spatial error, μ is specific effect and ε_{it} is a random term. Spatial error autocorrelation can be modeled in two ways. In the first approach, Baltagi et al. (2003), assumes that the error can be decomposed into individual effects and group effects independent of time and space, and the idiosyncratic error – spatially correlated shocks (innovations) (Millo & Piras, 2012). In the second approach, proposed by Kapoor et al. (2007), in the residual component both individual effects as well as the rest of the error are spatially correlated. All further models exploit the Baltagi error specification since the proposition of Kapoor error provided similar results of estimation.

The *lambda* coefficient (for spatial lag of dependent variable) in the estimated equation (1) is a measure of long-term integration of countries (Claeys et al., 2012), the correlation of the debt and it is also a measure of spatial persistence. This interpretation is permissible only if lambda turns out to be positive and significant. Additionally we have one more parameter for the spatial error lag which is denoted by *rho*. This *rho* coefficient has not been presented in the described formulas. The rho coefficient at spatial autocorrelation of the error term is treated as a short-term unobservable shock. When positive, it should be considered as the policy transmission parameter, but when negative, it can be interpreted as short-term adjustments and the indicator of competitive behavior of the government.

The individual, cross-sectional and time-wise panel effects are used to absorb the factors and patterns not included in the model. The cross-section factors (individual effects) include possible effects of: different policies (including the fiscal ones), different levels of openness and competitiveness, as well as social and market variables which are constant over time. Time effects allow for controlling of the shocks occurring within the territory, affecting all units simultaneously, such as the changes in global economic conditions (Romero & Burkey, 2011; Checherita-Westphal & Rother, 2011).

The crucial point in spatial analysis is to define the neighbors. The criterion most often applied to distinguish neighbors from not-neighbors is the contiguity of borders. Under this approach all regions sharing the same border are considered as neighbors. It is so called the first-order neighborhood. The basic weakness of this approach is that it does not allow for further-reaching interactions for example across the Europe. Thus, to deal with this problem the inverse distance matrix can be applied. This matrix includes all possible relations over the whole territory. In this approach the relations decay linearly with the distance and all regions are connected, however the impact of the most remote regions on the situation in a given country is weak. The modification of this approach involves the inverse of squared distance. This form of spatial weights ascertains the relation to decrease more than proportional with distance, giving closest neighbors stronger relations. It should be noted that the other spatial weights matrices are also possible. It includes: k-nearest neighbors, neighbors in distance of d-kilometers or the matrices based on socio-economic relations like the value of bilateral trade etc.

The dependent variable y_{it} is a function of explanatory variables and some specific terms:

Δ netLEND_BORROW2gdp = f(Wy, taxes, Δ taxes, capital market variables, debt, labor market variables, macroeconomic situation variables, households situation variables) + $\upsilon_i + \tau_t + u_{it}$
where u_{it}, υ_i, τ_t are described as in (2) and Δ is the denominator for variable changes (the difference of variable in two adhering years).

Specifically, the dynamic model has been estimated with endogenous and exogenous variables and surroundings, in the following form:

Δ netLEND_BORROW2gdp = f(W · Δ netLEND_BORROW2gdp, tauCONS, tauKAP, tauLABOR, Δ tauCONS, Δ tauKAP, Δ tauLABOR, Bondrate, Δ Bondrate, alfa, Herfindahl, INVESTpos, euroZONE, grossdebt2gdp, netLEND_BORROW2gdp, unemployment, Δ labor_prod, invest2gdp, gdp.growth.rate, export2gdp, import2gdp, domdem2gdp, savings2income, Δsavings2income) + $\upsilon_i + \tau_t + u_{it}$ (3)

Therefore the one-year change of the relative net debt (in relation to GDP) (ΔnetLEND_BORROW2gdp) is explained by the: relative level of net debt (netLEND_BORROW2gdp), annual changes in tax rates (Δ tauLABOR, Δ tauCONS, Δ tauCAP) and bond rates (Δ bondrate) and their levels (tauLABOR, tauCONS, tauCAP, Bondrate), economic and financial situation in the analysed year and changes in exogenous variables. One can expect that the change of labor tax (Δ tauLABOR) may result from a change in the tax rate on labor (tauLABOR), as well as changes in labor productivity (Δ labor_prod). A change in the consumption tax (Δ tauCONS) may be brought about by a change in the rate of the tax on consumption (tauCONS), as well as changes in consumption. The last can be at least partially explained by the change in the savings rate (Δ savings2-income). A change in the capital tax (Δ tauCAP) may be induced by a change of the capital tax rate (tauCAP), as well as changes in the productivity of capital. The latter should be related to the changes of interest rates on bonds (Δ bondrate). The macroeconomic environment is controlled by introduction of several variables like: the rate of unemployment (unemployment), the growth rate of GDP (gdp.growth.rate), savings relative to disposable income (savings2income) and exports, imports, domestic demand and investment in relation to GDP (export2gdp, import2gdp, grossdebt2gdp, domdem2gdp, invest2gdp). The situation on the financial market is expressed by the participation of residents in the ownership of capital (alpha), the degree of monopolization of the bank market (Herfindahl), the membership in the euro area in a given year as a dummy variable (euroZONE) and the investment position (INVESTpos) – the difference between a country's external financial assets and liabilities.

The spatial component was included twice in the model, firstly with the lagged spatial dependent variable and secondly with the spatially autoregressive residual component. Both components use the same spatial weights matrix W. Spatial weights matrix is build on the criterion of distance between centers of countries. The distances between countries stay constant in time and are exogenous. The two different spatial weights matrices W have been applied: inverse distance and squared inverse distance matrix. The use of distance matrices instead of contiguity measure stems from assumption that all countries in European area are strongly inter-related for economic, cultural and historical reasons, even if some of them are not the members of European Union. The contiguity matrix has been eliminated *ex ante*, because it includes only local neighborhood relations by common border, which oversimplifies the relations in Europe. Of the two variants of weights matrix, the simple inverse distance potentially better reflects the traditional tax competition with perfectly mobile capital but is not suitable to describe the real fiscal reaction of real economies, market imperfections and the prevalence of transaction cost. Much stronger links are assigned to closer countries with weights derived from squared inverse distance. This type of weights better reflects the possible agglomeration forces and differences in transactional costs. Additionally it facilitates the identification of local clusters with similar fiscal policies.

Calibration of the model (3) produced the estimates juxtaposed in the table of main result (Table 6). Finally the 5 models have been estimated. They included random effects (RE) models (1,3), fixed effects (FE) models (2,4), with inverse distance (W = 1/D) (3,4) and with squared-inverse distance (W = 1/D2) (1,2) and a-spatial OLS pooled model (5) to compare the results. The a-spatial model does not include: fixed or random effects, spatial weights matrix neither the panel structure. In a-spatial models the forecast of y ($\hat{y}$) is just the sum of products of the betas and explanatory variables. The best fitted model was the one with number 2 (with FE and inverse squared distance W), as the number of significant variables turns out to be the highest and AIC is better than in other models. It should be noted there are almost no tests for quality of spatial models and the final estimation decision is made on AIC and/or parameters like β, λ and ρ significance.

In all spatial models, spatial coefficients were significant and kept the same sign regardless of the type of model. Local dependence and local clusters are clearly visible in obtained results. Also some competitive mechanisms are present, what is indicated by negative spatial autocorrelation. Models with inverse squared distance spatial weights matrix W appeared to outperform models with inverse distance W. Also FE models were better than RE models in the significance of parameters.

Comparison of spatial models with a-spatial estimation suggests one interesting conclusion. GDP growth rate was significant only in a-spatial specification. Its positive impact can be seen only in a-spatial context when economies are treated as autarkies. However, when neighborhood relations are introduced, the impact of this variable becomes insignificant but other variables like tax rates, export and import, domestic demand become significant. This allows for concluding that listed variables cover the variability of GDP growth rate providing an additional international link. The second conclusion from OLS a-spatial estimation is that spatial FE models are closer to pooled estimations. It follows the postulate that spatial panel estimation should be an evolution not revolution to the OLS estimates. RE estimation produces much further results to the ones obtained in a-spatial pooled OLS as they have changed the signs of variables. This confirms that model number 2, with inverse-squared distance and Fixed Effects is the best fitted to the data. The model will be later called the final model. Besides this, result advocates for relation quickly decaying with distance which can indicate the weaker tax competition than postulated by traditional tax competition models and more close to the models with agglomeration effects.

Estimation was performed with **splm** package in the R CRAN software (Millo & Piras, 2012). Other spatial operations, like the construction of the spatial weights matrix and spatial lags, use **sp** package (Pebesma & Bivand, 2005), **spdep** (Bivand, 2013) or **maptools** (Bivand & Lewin-Koh, 2013).

Direct forecasts based on estimated coefficients would be impossible as the calibrated model includes spatial lag of dependent variable. It produces the feedback loop, when we try to explain y with spatial lag of y. Therefore it is necessary to apply the concept of impacts here. Table 7 reports those impacts. Share of direct and indirect impacts are about 50% of total impact, what means that half of effects of economic changes stay inside a given country, and the other half becomes the spillover which spreads to other countries.

Table 6: *Estimation results – the comparison.*

delta_netLEND_ BORROW2gdp	*Spatial panel model Baltagi error W = 1/D2*		*Spatial panel model Baltagi error W = 1/D*		*a-spatial OLS pooled model*
	1	2	3	4	5
	RE	FE	RE	FE	---
Intercept	85,83	---	90,80	---	99,79
delta_bondrate	0,130	-0,108	0,111	-0,158	0,172
bondrate	0,085	0,158	0,167	0,258*	0,187
delta_tauCONS	0,696***	0,801***	0,698***	0,760***	0,907***
delta_tauKAP	0,063*	0,096*	0,069	0,113*	0,112*
delta_tauLABOR	-0,025	0,165*	-0,011	0,183*	0,045
tauCONS	-0,116**	-0,310*	-0,086*	-0,288*	-0,031
tauKAP	-0,036*	-0,103*	-0,033*	-0,121**	-0,034
tauLABOR	0,007	-0,153*	0,003	-0,171*	-0,026
alfa	1,120	1,055	1,013	0,550	1,028
Herfindahl	-4,488*	-14,692*	-3,998*	-10,544	-4,309*
gdp.growth.rate	0,025	-0,010	0,027	-0,029	0,144*
unemployment	0,010	-0,061	0,020	0,039	0,038
euroZONE	-0,284	0,208	-0,288	0,323	-0,040
INVESTpos	-0,013***	-0,022**	-0,011**	-0,016*	-0,008*
export2gdp	-0,830	-1,637**	-0,904	-1,558*	-0,989
import2gdp	0,855	1,653**	0,931	1,595*	1,006
grossdebt2gdp	0,012*	0,068***	0,017**	0,072***	0,026***
domdem2gdp	-0,811	-1,581**	-0,878	-1,479*	-0,983
netLEND_ BORROW2gdp	0,300***	0,659***	0,314***	0,685***	0,322***
invest2gdp	-0,156***	-0,246***	-0,146**	-0,242**	-0,114*
savings2income	0,027	-0,002	0,041	0,0248	0,038
delta_labor_prod	0,075	0,196**	0,085	0,241**	0,255**
delta_savings2income	-0,036	-0,002	-0,031	-0,0014	-0,074
Phi (specific effects)	1,0e-08	---	1,0e-08	---	---
Rho (autocorrelation of error)	-0,927***	-0,811***	-0,999**	-1,142***	---
Lambda (spatial lag of y)	0,674***	0,481***	0,645***	0,432***	---

Source: Own calculation in R software.

After the calibration of the best fitted model (Fixed effect spatial panel model with Baltagi error) with impacts we conclude the following relations between changes in the debt and selected explanatory variables:

- related to consumption: a change in the tax on consumption (Δ tauCONS) the most strongly affects the change of net debt. The impact is positive and several times stronger than in the case of tax on capital (Δ tauCAP). The level of the tax rate of consumption (tauCONS) is also significant: the higher the tax rate on consumption, the weaker the change in the net debt. A change in the savings rate (Δ savings2income) does not affect the debt. It can justify the omission of savings in the theoretical models presented in previous chapters;

Table 7: *Impacts in spatial panel model with FE.*

delta_netLEND_BORROW-2gdp	*Spatial panel model FE Baltagi error W = 1/D2*		
	Direct	Indirect	Total
delta_bondrate	-0,109	-0,100	-0,209
bondrate	0,158	0,146	0,305
delta_tauCONS	0,805***	0,740***	1,545***
delta_tauKAP	0,097***	0,089***	0,186***
delta_tauLABOR	0,166*	0,153*	0,319***
tauCONS	-0,311***	-0,286***	-0,598***
tauKAP	-0,103***	-0,095***	-0,199***
tauLABOR	-0,153***	-0,141***	-0,295***
alfa	1,061	0,975	2,037
Herfindahl	-14,774***	-13,577***	-28,351***
gdp.growth.rate	-0,010	-0,009	-0,020
unemployment	-0,061	-0,056	-0,118
euroZONE	0,209	0,192	0,401
INVESTpos	-0,022***	-0,020***	-0,043***
export2gdp	-1,646***	-1,513***	-3,159***
import2gdp	1,662***	1,528***	3,191***
grossdebt2gdp	0,068***	0,063***	0,132***
domdem2gdp	-1,590***	-1,461***	-3,052***
netLEND_BORROW2gdp	0,662***	0,609***	1,271***
invest2gdp	-0,248***	-0,228***	-0,476***
savings2income	-0,002	-0,002	-0,005
delta_labor_prod	0,198***	0,181***	0,379***
delta_savings2income	-0,002	-0,002	-0,004

Source: Own calculation in R software.

- related to capital: a change in the tax on capital (Δ tauCAP) has a positive effect on the debt, although this effect is significantly weaker than in the case of the consumption tax. The level of the tax rate on capital (tauCAP) is also significant but this relationship is negative. A change in capital productivity (change in bond yields, Δ bondrate) does not matter for changes of the debt;
- related to labor market: all variables associated with labor (the level and changes in the labor tax rates and labor productivity: Δ tauLABOR, tauLABOR, Δ labor_prod) show a significant effect on the debt of countries. The effect is positive in the case of labor productivity changes and increasing the tax rate, and negative for the level of the tax rate;
- related to financial markets: the relative level of current debt (netLEND_BORROW2gdp) positively and significantly impacts the change in the debt. High monopolization of the banking sector (Herfindahl) and high investments position both in absolute and relative values (INVESTpos, invest2gdp) significantly reduce the changes of debt;
- related to debt: the balance of debt is important for the dynamics of debt changes. Both the gross state budget deficit to GDP (grossdebt2gdp) and net government borrowing relative to GDP (netLEND_BORROW2gdp) have a significant and positive impact on the debt changes. This confirms the existence of a vicious circle of the debt: countries strongly indebted indebt faster than countries with low debt.

Implications of this model are as follows: all tax rates (as level) impact significantly and negatively changes of the debt. It means that higher rates imply the lower changes of debt. This result is consistent with the observation from the theoretical static model with agglomeration forces, because it confirms that higher tax rates stabilize the fiscal policy before the changes of the debt. However, also all changes of tax rates (deltas) impact significantly and positively changes of debt. It means that the changes of debt are correlated with the changes of tax rates and they occur in the same direction. Impact of tax rates changes is the strongest in case of tax on consumption (three times stronger than tax on capital and double than tax on labor). Selected model proves the significant and strong spillover effects, which are in the same direction as local in-the-country effects. Spatial framework suggests that both debt as well as taxes and other significant variables follow spatial patterns. Those spatial patterns assume stronger relations between direct contiguity neighbors and closely located countries; however they also include overall European interactions.

5. The implications from the model results for the tax-mix

Direct and indirect impacts estimated for the final model specification show that mostly direct and indirect impacts are of the same magnitude. Final influence of given variable on debt performance in circa 50% acts in given country, and in circa 50% in neighboring countries.

On the basis of the estimated impacts the simulation of possible changes can be performed. We assumed slight changes, namely the decrease of tax rates by 1 percentage point from the average level of given tax rate for the whole sample. Ceteris paribus, we can observe the impact of this change on debt. All the changes will impact through two coefficients: on level (tau) and change (delta_tau). The statistics of tax rates and debt are given in Table 8.

Table 8: *Descriptive statistics for tax rates and debt.*

	tauCONS	*tauKAP*	*tauLABOR*	*netLEND_BORROW2gdp*
Min.	12.60	5.50	0.00	-30.864
1st Qu.	18.70	20.20	31.57	-4.570
Median	21.32	24.85	34.29	-2.510
Mean	21.77	25.10	34.05	-2.266
3rd Qu.	24.20	29.02	37.85	-0.142
Max.	34.20	49.90	43.80	18.787

Source: Own analysis on data from EUROSTAT and IMF

Below are the predictions based on the direct and indirect impact coefficients.

1) Change in the tax on capital: we assume that tauCAP will drop from 34% to 33% (what means that delta_tauCAP = -1).

   impact of change (delta): direct + indirect = 0,097 * (-1) + 0,089 * (-1) = -0,186
   impact of level: direct + indirect = -0,103 * (-1) + (-0,095) * (-1) = 0,198
   impact on given location: 0,097 * (-1) - 0,103 * (-1) = 0,006
   impact on neighbors: 0,089 * (-1) - 0,095 * (-1) = 0,006
   total impact: 0,012

This means that lowering tax rate on capital by 1 p.p. will decrease debt to GDP in total by 0.012 p.p., of which by 0.006 p.p. in a given country and by 0.006 in neighboring countries. The positive sign of the impact is determined by the higher reaction on the level of capital tax rate than the effect induced by tax rate changes. The latter effect is negative.

2) Change in the tax on labor: we assume that tauLABOR will drop from 24% to 23% (what means delta_tauLABOR = -1).

impact of change (delta): direct + indirect = 0,166 * (-1) + 0,153 * (-1) = -0,319
impact of level: direct + indirect = -0,153 * (-1) + (-0,141) * (-1) = 0,295
impact on given location: 0,166 * (-1) - 0,153 * (-1) = -0,013
impact on neighbors: 0,153 * (-1) - 0,141 * (-1) = -0,012
total impact: -0,025

This means that lowering tax rate on labor by 1 p.p. will increase debt to GDP in total by 0.025 p.p., of which by 0.013 p.p. in a given country and by 0.012 in neighboring countries. For the labor tax the effect triggered by tax rates changes overwhelms the effect of level providing negative total impact.

3) Change in the tax on consumption: we assume that tauCONS will drop from 24% to 23% (what is equivalent of delta_tauCONS = -1).

impact of change (delta): direct + indirect = 0,805 * (-1) + 0,740 * (-1) = -1,545
impact of level: direct + indirect=-0,311*(-1) + (-0,286) * (-1) = 0,598
impact on given location: 0,805 * (-1) - 0,311 * (-1) = -0,494
impact on neighbors: 0,740 * (-1) - 0,286 * (-1) = -0,454
total impact: -0,948

This means that lowering tax rate on consumption by 1 p.p. will increase debt to GDP in total by 0.95 p.p., by 0.5 p.p. in a given country and by 0.45 in neighboring countries. Once again the total impact is negative.

Although the model estimates positive forecast of the tax rate on capital, but the size of this effect is very weak (166:1). The impact of labor tax is twice as high as that estimated on capital, but still weak (80:1) and negative (decreasing a taxation on labor increases debt). The strongest impact is observed in case of consumption tax. Economies in the last case are expected to react very strongly, because 1 p.p. change induces the change of the debt by 0.5 p.p. (which means the relation 2:1) in the opposite direction. Therefore the policy of increasing consumption tax and labor tax with decrease of capital taxation can be perceived the best in debt reduction.

6. Conclusions

In the introduction we set few questions to be answered. Below, with summarizing the results described in details in this chapter, we will try to answer those questions.

When considering whether fiscal policy changes are inter-related between countries and over time, the answer for this question is positive. It has been proven that all taxes follow spatial patterns in levels as well as in changes. Multivariate statistics analysis proved that even though the fiscal policy is not integrated, it is autonomously synchronized over time and tax changes over time are highly correlated. What's more, it is correlated over space. In geographical groups the convergence of tax rates is observed. Especially, taxes on consumption follow patterns assumed by geographical clusters of countries.

We can also answer in a positive way to the question whether there are any spatial spillover effects in transmission of tax rate changes to other countries. Spatial spillover effects were proved in econometric modeling and they are responsible for about 50% of the whole effect observed on the debt changes. Calculated spatial parameters of the model and spatially interpreted coefficients (direct and indirect impacts) give clear evidence, that spatial patterns are strong in both taxes and debt. We can also state the nature of those spillovers. Modeling proved that interactions between countries are stronger than proportionally to the distance. This means that there exists local clubs of reactions. Obviously there exist general linkages between all European countries.

Chapter 5
Fiscal policy recommendations

European corporate income tax rates are now one of the lowest in the world[24] especially if considered by regions. It should be emphasized that in recent years the trend of declining capital tax rates is common and the most countries decided to lower them in last decade regardless of the impact of financial crisis. However, these cuts usually were followed by the tax base broadening. This process is especially evident in developed economies but debatable in developing economies. It is guessed that governments decrease corporate tax rates to attract or keep multinationals operating in the countries. For example in the case of United Kingdom the corporate tax rate dropped from 52% in 1980 to 28% in 2008 and finally 20% in 2015. Simultaneously government spending is not so easy to cut which exerts pressure on the financing with higher taxes on labor and consumption. The latter tax rate does not experience dramatic decline in last decade. The labor tax rates in the European countries decreased slightly after the outburst of the financial crisis and consumption tax rates even increased. The reason for this seems natural: as multinationals and capital are highly mobile and can easily move to other countries, the labor and consumption are perceived as relatively inelastic and prone to higher taxation. Therefore facing little danger of massive tax avoidance the increase of tax burden on labor or consumption is preferred from economic and political reasons. Especially current fiscal policy focus on the consumption tax rates because they can provide additional tax revenues without imposing significant distortion to the economy (we left aside the diminishing redistribution effect caused by the regressivity of this kind of taxation). The labor taxation is chosen less likely as a source of additional revenue because it can adversely affect employment. It is also not popular for political reasons because voters are not willing to support the policy of labor taxation increase.

The fiscal policy recommendation can be discussed in the short and in the long term as well as from the theoretical and empirical point of view. In the theoretical static model the short term adjustment should take into account the maximization of citizen welfare with protection of fiscal solvency of governments. We cannot propose the policy recommendations focused solely on the revenue maximization in the short term. Such a policy, although effective in obtaining the solvency and

24 Tax foundation site http://taxfoundation.org/

high revenues for budgets, could significantly impair the well-being of citizen and probably would not be sustainable in the long term. In the long term the revenue maximization policy should not be so harmful, because the government has to take care of the increase of tax bases used for tax revenue collection. This means that the taxes cannot be too high in the long term even if the only purpose of the government is to collect the highest level of budgetary revenues. In the short term pressures of tax competition and strategic actions of other governments may have a significant impact the equilibrium tax rates. Reversely, in the long term these factors are less troublesome for establishment of an optimal tax policy. Additionally, the focus on budget revenues maximization in the long term more closely corresponds to the concept of fiscal solvency. For these reasons, our static models differ from dynamic one in the form of objective functions and in the description of countries reaction on tax changes that occurred abroad. In the simpler one-country model the reaction of government is limited and triggered by the changes in foreign and home trans-border purchases and by the capital income shifting. In the two-country static analysis the change involves the Nash equilibrium of tax rates and bonds and the reaction to the situation emerging in other country. In the dynamic model the target levels of taxation and government bonds issuance are observed from the perspective of a single country, so the solution is more similar to the first version of the static model.

From an empirical point of view, tax adjustments include countries in remote locations. This is evidenced by the presence of significant spatial effects among the European countries in regression explaining the changes of debt. Perhaps this phenomenon is intensified in the crisis period. During economic prosperity the most important relationships occur between neighbors and tax rates behavior tends to cluster. This is confirmed by the superior fit of the model using inverse squared distance with high spillover effect on the changes of debt changes. Obviously this result can be a consequence of an actual tax competition on tax bases or a follower effect. However, the effect is decreasing with distance which rather stipulates not universal impact of tax incentives on tax bases. The econometric result suggests that location proximity of competing tax jurisdiction has a greater effect than global factors. It precludes the traditional explanations of tax burden behavior driven exclusively by tax competition or competition with agglomeration effects.

Ordinary tax competition presupposes impact on arbitrarily large distances (because the cost of capital transfer is zero) but it does not consider the presence of local effects. On the other hand tax competition with agglomeration effects postulates the high impact of transaction costs decaying with a distance. The latter effect may explain the occurrence of local effects but excludes the long distance effects because tax competition on long distance should disappear when agglomeration forces are present. If the cost of capital transfer depends on the distance then the interactions of tax rates and debt should be stronger among neighbors. Econometric results show that the tax impact is almost perfectly divided between country and vicinity. Moreover this spillover effect has similar amplitude as changes implied by internal – country factors. Therefore there are at least two explanations: either the tax competition is weak or external factors determine the value of taxes in the response for the government debt increase. This result is very important because it curbs the tax competition impact to only short distances. Additionally high level of taxation decreases the vulnerability of tax adjustment to the debt changes. This stays in line with prediction of the two-country static model with agglomeration forces.

According to the results of the econometric model, the observed tax adjustment – related to the deterioration of fiscal solvency – includes the largest changes in consumption tax and relatively moderate changes in the taxes on capital and labor. This is consistent with the expectation of limited impact on the debt caused by distortionary taxes (these imposed on capital or labor) when the adjustment of consumption tax is available. Correlation analysis indicates positive relation between different types of tax rates and their changes. This is also confirmed by the analysis of spatial impacts. The tax rates levels affect debt changes negatively whereas the changes of tax rates – positively. High taxation in a given country decreases the possibility of the insolvency problem occurrence. At the same time it makes more probable the reaction of tax rates on the increase of debt to be positive. This result strengthens the conclusion that all three types of taxes are complementary but not substitutive. The short-term fiscal adjustments draw all taxes in the same direction when the sovereign debt is growing. The adjustment consists in the tax burden lifting.

The taxation of capital may be an exception, which in the econometric model exhibits a very small but positive impact on the level of debt. Perhaps countries with relatively good credibility may increase the taxation of capital (rather than decrease it), because they become an attractive place for capital investment, when fiscal solvency of individual countries diversifies. Probably these countries are characterized by high level of capital taxation. Therefore in their situation the best policy can involve the reduction of capital taxation which does not worsen their solvency. In the case of countries with lower taxation the effect of tax rates changes can be prevailing and capital tax rates should be increased. If we abstain from the differences in situation of particular countries then the optimal tax response on the debt increase should include the higher tax rates on consumption and labor with capital tax rates unchanged or slightly decreased. The presented explanation of capital tax adjustment is not unique, for example the government's behavior can be simply consistent with tax competition theory under which lower taxation attracts capital and allows for higher tax revenue collection of all taxes. Capital taxation differs from taxation of labor and consumption which are not linked with external effects of capital flows. Finally, lower tax rate on capital should contribute to the reduction of debt ratio to GDP as observed in the results of empirical study.

It is worth to note that econometric result does not disprove the findings of two static models presented in the second chapter. In the one-country model the basic adjustment should be made on labor taxation whereas the effect on capital tax is ambiguous. The consumption tax is driven by the reactions of purchases on home-country taxation. This could be relatively small in practice, because of the high transaction costs with important role played by transportation cost. In the two-country model the Nash equilibrium provides similar results only when the domestic shares of portfolio and direct investments are relatively high (the economy is relatively closed) or the foreign direct investments are relatively high (the economy is a developing one)[25]. In these two cases we expect ambiguous changes of capital taxation and the increase of labor tax rates as a reaction on the debt increase[26]. As in the one-country model the consumption tax should be affected by exogenous factors but this time it would be connected with the size of shadow economy instead of cross-border purchases. This consequence is not surprising because the cross-border purchases are now modeled as fully endogenous. For moderate size of the shadow economy there is possibility to increase consumption tax and to hamper the increase of two other tax rates (on labor and consumption). Low level of non-residents direct investment urges the need for higher labor taxation in response for debt enlargement. In the second regime when direct investment is possessed by domestic residents but portfolio investment is international, the reaction of capital tax is clear and positive but the reaction of labor becomes inconclusive. However this case is not supported by the empirical findings in spatial panel study (we are not observing this kind of adjustment).

---

25 It corresponds to the first regime of tax rates change in two-country static model.

26 It seems interesting that this result is opposite to the postulate of optimal taxation in a closed economy. The taxation of capital should be high in a closed economy because capital is immobile. However our model does not replicate the closed economy because there are cross borders purchases of goods and capital investments (direct and portfolio). This two factors plus the necessity for obtaining Nash equilibrium alter the expected adjustment of capital tax rates in the two countries world making the capital taxation not so obvious.

One cannot preclude that relatively limited changes of labor taxation can arise from conflicting goals strived by countries affected by the last crisis. These objectives include the protection of: private demand, jobs and fiscal solvency. Typically, in the first phase of the crisis, governments preferred to lower tax rates on labor in order to stimulate employment (or discourage unemployment). Such a policy can be effective as long as the crisis does not last too long and when there is no risk of country's insolvency. If the crisis lingers, the increase in labor taxation can be found as a solution facilitating the recovery of the governments' creditworthiness, even at the cost of higher unemployment. The legitimacy of such a policy depends on the dynamics of the crisis and its duration.

The crisis of 2008 began as a financial crisis and over time transformed into a debt crisis. This confined the choice of optimal fiscal policies by governments. It seems that if the crisis from the beginning had been the debt crisis (with the threat of countries' insolvency and the problem with debt refinancing) then the best reply for government would be to increase the burden of all three taxes, with the special emphasis put on consumption tax. This would prevent the significant changes in the tax burden causing distortion of consumption and production. Unfortunately, the nature of the crisis has been altered with time and the fiscal policy's response in the first stage of the crisis was concentrated on the preservation of jobs but not on solvency. This implied the initial decrease of taxes affecting production factors (like taxes on capital and labor) observed in the raw data.

Some results, like for example the higher spatial effects between closed neighbors or relatively insensitivity of countries with higher taxation on the exacerbation of debt problem can hint the existence of agglomeration effects. The latter would imply the inevitability of differentiated tax policies for countries lying in the vicinity but not for the all countries from the sample. The agglomeration effects occurence provides evidence against the common tax harmonization on the pan-European level. In the same time it does not preclude the presence of tax competition inside the cluster of countries instead of the competition involving the all countries on the continent.

In most debates, papers and books, country economies and fiscal policies are treated as independent and only inferred by such phenomena like fiscal or tax competition. It is hard to find an approach which would emphasize European regional similarities as a factor significantly affecting the country fiscal policy. As the empirical spatial econometric study proves, European economies are neither independent nor fully integrated on the continent scale. European economies play their fiscal policies in regional groups covering at most few closely located countries. This geographical proximity is of crucial importance for inter-country fiscal coordination because the long distance effects seem to be relatively small.

Nevertheless the occurrence of effects covering all investigated countries, revealed in the econometric study, may either suggest the ineffectiveness of country tax policies. This means that the best level for the implementation of common fiscal initiative would be the regional level (neither pan-European nor country). The tendency for fiscal policy clustering does not exclude the possibility of discussion over the selected forms of tax policy harmonization.

Despite the developed models do not cover full fiscal union (the fiscal consolidation) in European Union, we should notice that debate in Europe on fiscal union is still sounding[27]. There are plenty of arguments for and against fiscal consolidation[28]. Inter alia reasons against consolidation base on the autonomy rule and the free rider problem. In democracies, inseparably connected with local level, societies do not want to lose the flexibility and responsibility in managing their own problems. There is also problem of inter-country cultural differences causes, that thrifty and decent societies will pay more under fiscal union on behalf of financially non-rigorous and lavish societies. The motives against are directed in greater extend inward, anchored on local scale and with social overtone. Arguments for fiscal union follow the economic rationale of building the economic competitiveness in the world business environment. The fiscal union supporters concern the need for effective economic competition with Asian, American and African economies and better management of the euro currency area in the turbulent times. These reasons are perceived as: outward oriented, expressed in technocratic style and build in with global and not local perspective.

It should not be forgotten that full fiscal integration requires to deal with differences in country-level prices. For example high tax rates can be justified for corporate taxation when average salaries are low. The high taxation of labor is reasonable if the remuneration of employees is high but countries vary with the labor costs. The high salary in one country can be perceived as low in another. From OECD 2013 survey of average labor cost (Pomerleau, 2014), the average total tax wedge is estimated at 35,8% with differences ranging from 55,8% in Belgium, through 35,6% in Poland to 26,6% in Ireland. In the same time, the average labor cost in Belgium is about 73000 USD, in Poland 26800 USD and in Ireland about 44500 USD. The income after taxation is in the opposite order than implied by tax wedge which can undermine the idea of uniform taxation. Thus, not only tax rates, but also the size of tax base plays an important role in setting

27 Debating Europe site: http://www.debatingeurope.eu/

28 Currently, state of fiscal integration in Europe is that indirect taxes and excise duties are to some degree harmonized and direct taxes have some cross-border issues fixed.

fiscal policy. Implementing full fiscal integration in Europe in terms of uniform tax rates would require at start the integration of wages to equalize tax base and to average the labor cost. However the latter requirements can be counterproductive.

Instead of full fiscal integration we can consider the tax base harmonization with formula apportionment. However, this proposition provides several drawbacks regardless the pattern of income assignment and the voluntariness or the compelling participation in the reform. In the literature the basic argument against applies to the facilitation of tax avoidance by the replacement of efforts for taxable income reduction with efforts concentrated on the artificial formation of income-split-factors. The very important is also the selection of factors used for formula apportionment. The highest increase in tax burden is expected if sales are used for the income split and the lowest when income split between jurisdictions bases on assets. In order to ensure the neutrality of the tax reform for budgetary revenues the most likely is the use of several factors at the same time. Unfortunately several factors complicate the structure of new regulations and require the choice of weights for each factor. The latter can trigger political controversies and lead to obstruction of the project. Summing up the current criticism of this approach covers: a possible decline in tax revenues after the introduction of common tax base (due to the compensation of losses and possible voluntary participation in the new tax instrument), administrative difficulties (due to the lack of centralized tax authority responsible for revenue transfers between countries at European level) and the changes in the tax avoidance pattern from income-reduction oriented forms into forms concentrated on the modification of selected factors associated with the formula apportionment. Generally the latter type of tax avoidance is considered as more difficult to control than simple income-reduction-strategies. Last but not least is the fear of lower level of tax control at national level triggered by the broken relation between tax revenues and control efforts.

The short term model presented in Chapter 2 pinpoints some arguments against the common tax base. The harmonization of tax bases, if labor is immobile, makes feasible subsidization of capital and strong taxation of labor. It should be emphasized that this conclusion applies to all three considered cases, namely the income split based on: capital income, labor income or a fixed exogenous ratio. Although the proposed model does not allow for a direct examination of other ways of formula apportionment, such as consumption or value added, it seems that all propositions should mimic the result obtained for the three considered cases. Each solution ought to be characterized by negative capital taxation and positive taxation of labor. This result stems directly from the mobility of capital combined with the immobility of labor and with positive impact of capital accumulated in the country on labor productivity. In these circumstances countries can limit international mobility of capital providing the subsidy for capital and taxing the enlarged labor income. Support for capital increases the remuneration of labor and allows for higher labor taxation in each country. The sketched mechanism would intensify the tax competition and certainly it would not be helpful in curbing too low capital taxation.

In the case of European Union low labor mobility between Union members and the rest of the world is incontestable. Even if labor mobility between countries forming the Union would be substantial, the labor mobility outside of the integration area would be negligible due to the large geographical size and large population of countries involved in tax harmonization initiative. The movements inside the Union are greater than migrations outside the European community. The introduction of a third party, not covered by the harmonization should also confirm obtained simulation results, because capital subsidization contributes to the inflow of capital to countries applying formula apportionment. However, contrary to the intentions, this type of policy should not stop the tendency to the "race to the bottom" in capital taxation and even it exacerbates this phenomenon. The strongest capital subsidies should be applied when the distribution of income would be determined on the basis of exogenous relation of capital invested in given countries and the smallest when the distribution of income refers to the distribution of labor income. Regardless of the chosen method of formula apportionment, the concept of a common tax base leads to a waste of resources and remains interior to the full tax harmonization. For this reason, this policy should not be recommended.

If common tax base had been used during the debt crisis, the variable share of residents' participation in capital would exert some pressure on the level of taxation. The decrease of foreign investors share in government bonds (de-internalization process consisting in the transition from second to the first regime of the two-country static model solution) should strengthen the subsidization of capital financed from higher taxation of labor. This is consistent with a prediction that the formation of capital should be more supported by country government when capital in the country belongs mainly to residents than when it is possessed largely by non-residents. Reversely it means that this conclusion can be treated as a kind of export tax burden hypothesis proof, when the share of foreign investors in domestic capital enlarges. In the latter situation the reason for capital subsidization is hampered which lead to lesser subsidization (or greater taxation) of capital.

An interesting issue, related to the use of a common tax base, refers to the changes caused by debt and more specifically by the changes in debt servicing costs. Increase of the latter in a country should reduce the subsidization of capital and increase the burden on labor. This last prediction follows directly from the need to ensure fiscal solvency. Paradoxically, problems with debt as well as an increase of income from capital shifted abroad could restrict unnecessary subsidization of capital and then improve the improper fiscal policy. The described analysis is correct as far as we assume that it is impossible to adjust taxes on consumption. If such adjustment is available or if a government can receive any other additional tax revenue (for example from transaction tax), then the problem of capital subsidization would be aggravated. Although the additional source of budgetary revenues can ease the labor tax burden. In the considered static model any taxation providing tax revenues acts similarly to so call "lump sum tax" – the tax which provides no distortion to the economy.

A slightly different conclusions come with the concept of transaction tax (sometimes identified with financial transaction tax) imposed on financial transactions or transaction of financial market. Despite the limitation of the main static model (which is not well suited to analyze the taxation imposed only on secondary financial market purchases) one can expect the lower taxation of labor after imposition of transaction tax from reasons mentioned above. Besides transaction tax should be symmetric (e.g. introduced in both countries with the same rate) because in asymmetric case the taxation of labor would be forced to increase in the country without such a tax (or with lower transaction tax). The impact of transaction tax on capital taxation depends on the tax regime. In ordinary situation (second regime) the imposition of transaction tax (perceived as income tax on net income from bonds) decreases capital taxation. The same introduction of the new tax works differently when the internalization becomes weaker and the economy switches to the first regime. For higher level of resident share in capital and portfolio investment the taxation of capital can be higher with, than without transaction tax. This means, that if the policymakers objective is to decrease the tax burden on labor during the crisis then the harmonized transaction tax on net bonds income can be considered as a correct instrument. However, it would not be an effective tool in shaping lower capital taxation. The last conclusion is implied by the ambiguous sign of capital tax reaction on debt level. The latter is caused by the changes of portfolio and direct investments internalization.

For other versions of transaction tax (which involves taxation of debt service costs or income received from the new bonds issuance) the sustainable application of such policies could significantly affect future ability of government to issue securities. For example, a partial debt cancellation would help to reduce the tax burden necessary to repay the bonds but it can discourage investors to subsequent bonds purchases. Therefore, this form of transaction tax seems to be undesirable at least in the long term. It is a consequence of constant level of government sales of bonds assumed in the two-country static model. However, in practice the possibility of bonds market placement is very limited for governments with low credibility. Ignoring this effect, taxes or bonds issuance could strongly affect the tax burden on capital and labor. The proposal very similar to the financial transaction tax is the tax imposed on debt servicing cost. Such a tax could serve as a tool directly limiting costs of debt and indirectly improving tax revenues. These conclusions are independent of restraining the speculative bonds abuse postulated in the economic literature on the topic. In fact, it is doubtful whether a small rate of this tax could prevent a mass sell-off bonds leading to a decline in their prices and to increase of its profitability. This is especially evident if we deal with highly motivated investors who fear of country default risk.

According to the simulation analysis, from available scrutinized options, the greatest benefit could bring the imposition of financial transactions tax. Contrary to this, the harmonization of capital tax bases should be regarded as disadvantageous regardless of the chosen formula apportionment (the formula of corporate income split between jurisdictions). Unfortunately the consequences of full capital tax harmonization are quite difficult to assess, eliminating the need for capital inflow subsidization and the introduction of mechanism of revenue redistribution on the European Union level (like for example formula apportionment). In the light of simulations of tax bases harmonization, the full harmonization of capital taxation can be perceived as better than any kind of tax base harmonization with formula apportionment. But it does mean that this form of fiscal policy should be recommended. Generally, the harmonization of capital tax base with formula apportionment inevitably leads to subsidization of capital and taxation of labor. This is a consequence of increasing labor productivity with capital inflow and the omission of possibility of capital or labor outflow outside the area of harmonized tax base. Low taxation of capital although ineffective could bring the enlarged income for labor and then can be retrieved by governments without afraid of the tax base escape.

In dynamic model one can observe quite different pattern of interdependences than in the static model. This diversity of results can be explained in two ways; firstly by the another form of objective function concerning the maximization of government revenue in the long term instead of maximization of the consumers' utility, as in the static model. Although these objectives seem to be quite different, but they are not precluding each other, since the maximizing revenues government cannot diminish the tax bases in the long term. Therefore the solutions of the dynamic model define the maximum level of tax burden that may be imposed on society. If the government instead of revenue maximization would choose the maximization of citizen's utility then the fiscal solvency constraint cannot be met. Second reason of incompatibility between the static models is another mechanism of decision-making. In the static model many macroeconomic parameters are constant. This allows for charging taxes on tax bases that cannot easily escape abroad. For example, the capital income can be highly taxed because only the fixed portion of them is transferred abroad and the rest remains implicit to the tax authorities. Obviously, because levels of taxation in simulation have to describe the Nash equilibrium, the most important factor affecting taxes is a reaction of a foreign government on the changes in home taxation. Respectively, the dynamic model describes a situation seen only from a position of distinguished country with indirect impact of international tax competition. In the dynamic model, despite assumption of constant level of income shifting, the level of capital invested is variable. Finally, the static model treats the tax on consumption as constant and determined by the exogenous factors. In the dynamic model the consumption tax is only partially predetermined by the relative size of explicit consumption to the implicit one. This extends the model including the concept of shadow economy with the part of total consumption.

The basic recommendations of dynamic model are implied by the behavior of several selected parameters. First we can observe the effect of the explicit consumption share on the tax rates. Countries with higher share of explicit consumption can tax higher capital and consumption. Therefore the tax revenues of the government depend on the possibility of shadow economy curbing. This can be linked with the possibility of efficient enforcement or welfare of given country. Affluent countries and strong governments should tax consumption and capital higher. This mimics the effect of financial compensation postulated by D. Swank (1998) and provided by governments to prevent the economic instability caused by globalization. Despite the similar outcome the mechanism behind this is quite different and applies directly to the possibilities but not to the (economical or political) needs.

It should be noted that consumption and capital taxation are complementary if the consumption is shrinking. The labor taxation seems to be neutral. In other words, it means that when the explicit consumption decreases (the shadow economy is inflating) – the taxation of consumption should be reduced in the first place (and with the highest rate-cut) and subsequently it should be followed by capital taxation. Lower revenues from these two taxes should result in declining sovereign debt. Subsequently this should trigger the drop of bonds issuance to fulfill the fiscal solvency constraint. In this situation the compensation of tax revenues decline with higher labor taxation is pointless, because it would strongly reduce the labor supply in equilibrium.

The reaction of consumption depends on the size of the shadow economy. The numerical result indicates that the highest consumption in the long term occurs when explicit consumption accounts for about 85% of the total consumption. (With a different set of values in the numerical simulation the consumption is maximized for explicit consumption reaching about 75%). The tax structure in this point would require the highest taxation on labor, then on consumption and in third place on capital. This structure resembles taxation in developed countries, where labor taxation plays the more important role than the consumption taxation. This result is important if one can want to obtain the maximum consumption available inside the optimal fiscal policy aimed to budget revenue maximization. In general the optimal policy should concentrate on the control of accepted level of untaxed (implicit) consumption maximizing the total consumption (both explicit and implicit). This result is interesting because set some limits on the size of shadow economy becoming the synonym of explicit consumption.

The level of country debt is also an important issue. At high wage level the policy recommendation would be to maintain higher debt level, regardless of the values of optimal tax rates. This problem is intensified if labor taxes strongly reduce the labor supply. In the latter case, we can try to decrease the taxation of labor and respectively the level of debt. Another solution requires all of three taxes to be fixed with significant reduction of debt. The increase of debt can be assessed positively but only if consumption and capital are not deteriorating. The former can escape to the shadow economy and the latter can avoid taxation by income shifting. These effects are the most likely when the return on capital is high or capital shifting activity is small. This can be the case of a closed economy with low capital endowment. In an open economy higher indebtedness could be optimal and do not interfere with formation of production factors.

Other results are in line with expectations. Debt should increase whenever tax revenues increase or when investor's tolerance for the size of tax revenues to the proxy of production is higher. This policy simply limits the need for tax raise and allows pursuing higher levels of public spending by government. In good times the strategy of higher debt generation should dominate the tax increasing strategies simply as a cheaper solution. It should be noted that in practice we do not know what determines the tolerance of investors to the governments' debt level. This is crucial to comprehend the notion of fiscal solvency. Probably it is at least partly determined by psychological factors and partly by speculative reason. The latter is due to the observation of trends on the debt market, the anticipation of cost of debt service and last but not least – the possibilities of debt refinancing. It does not exclude that in the case of low credibility, the increase of all tax rates, despite the lack of the revenue increase, may calm the negative sentiment on the market and limit debt servicing costs in the short term. The parameter of debt tolerance affects positively all state variables (capital, labor and consumption) because it allows for higher indebtedness. It should be emphasized that this parameter is neutral to tax rates. This means that if the investors on financial market accept higher level of bonds issuance then the fiscal policy could be completely passive. Therefore in the long term we should not react on the debt tolerance with tax rates changes.

Tax shirking is irrelevant for taxation of consumption and labor but intensively affects taxation of capital. Higher shifting provides higher capital taxation because government tries to compensate the loss of revenues. Such a policy has very serious implication because it hampers the stock of capital and in the next step – the consumption. As a consequence the share of labor increases but it is not sufficient to prevent the drop of consumption. Nevertheless such a policy can be regarded as effective in debt service financing. Thus, it appears that limitation of income shifting abroad is the one of the necessary requirements ensuring high level of consumption, taxation and bonds issuance. This is true even if the government's objective is to maximize revenue rather than utility (welfare or well-being) of its citizens. It should be noted that this conclusion of the model is not very different of prediction implied by the static model.

The impact of interest rate on: capital, labor and consumption are not astonishing as well. The increasing interest rate decreases the level of capital and consumption in equilibrium. Simultaneously the level of labor is increasing so one can notice the substitution of capital with labor in the equilibrium. We can expect that higher cost of capital is responsible for smaller utilization of this production factor. This is confirmed by the tax rates behavior because the only tax rate which is affected by interest is a capital tax rate. The rate decreases with the interest rate and lower level of invested capital. Finally the budgetary situation should be quite good because the level of bond is higher which should coexist with higher credibility of government. It is worth to note that the reaction of economy on increasing tax shifting and increasing interest rate is similar and leads to greater utilization of labor in the equilibrium.

According to results of dynamic model the optimal fiscal policy requires the higher taxation of capital when capital is in abundance. The consumption taxation can be high only when shadow economy is not large. Finally, labor taxation can be set independently to the other tax rates and its level should be determined by the income effect modifying the long term labor supply.

References

Aiyagari, S. R. 1994. Uninsured idiosyncratic risk and aggregate saving, *Quarterly Journal of Economics* 109 (3): 659-684.

Albanesi, S., and Sleet, C. 2006. Dynamic optimal taxation with private information, *Review of Economic Studies* 73 (1): 1-30.

Altshuler, R., and Grubert, H. 2010. Formula apportionment: Is it better than the current system and are there better alternatives?, *National Tax Journal* 63 (4): 1145-1184.

Aronsson, T., Löfgren, K-G., and Sjögren, T. 2001. Union wage setting and capital income taxation in dynamic general equilibrium, *German Economic Review* 2 (2): 141-175.

Atkinson, A. B., and Stiglitz, J. E. 1980. *Lectures on public economics*, New York: McGraw-Hill.

Auerbach, A. J, and Hines Jr., J. R. 2001. Taxation and economic efficiency, NBER Working Paper 8181.

Baldacci E., Dell'Erba S., Poghosyan T., 2011. Spatial spillovers in emerging market spreads, IMF Working Paper WP/11/221, http://www.imf.org/external/pubs/ft/wp/2011/wp11221.pdf

Baldwin, R., and Krugman, P. 2004. Agglomeration, integration and tax harmonization, *European Economic Review* 48 (1): 1-23.

Baldwin, R., and Okubo, T. 2009. Tax reform, delocation and heterogeneous firms, *The Scandinavian Journal of Economics* 111 (4): 741-764.

Baltagi, B. H., Song, S. H., Koh, W. (2003), Testing panel data regression models with spatial error correlation, *Journal of Econometrics*, 117, 123-150.

Becker, J., and Fuest, C. 2010. Tax enforcement and tax havens under formula apportionment, *International Tax and Public Finance* 17 (3): 217-235.

Bellak, C., Leibrecht, M., and Damijan J. 2009. Infrastructure endowment and corporate income taxes as determinants of foreign direct investment in central and Eastern European countries, *The World Economy* 32 (2): 267-290.

Bénassy-Quéré, A., Gobalraja, N., and Trannoy, A. 2007. Tax and public input competition, *Economic Policy* 22 (50): 385-430.

Bivand, R. S. 2013. *spdep: Spatial dependence: weighting schemes, statistics and models*. R package version 0.5-65.

Bivand, R. S., and Lewin-Koh, N. 2013. *maptools: Tools for reading and handling spatial objects*. R package version 0.8-27.

Borck, R., and Pflüger, M. 2006. Agglomeration and tax competition, *European Economic Review* 50 (3): 647-668.

Bordignon M., Cerniglia F., Revelli F. 2003. In search of yardstick competition: a spatial analysis of Italian municipality property tax setting, *Journal of Urban Economics* 54: 199-217

Bretschger, L., and Hettich, F. 2002. Globalization, capital mobility and tax competition: Theory and evidence for OECD countries, *European Journal of Political Economy* 18 (4): 695-716.

Brueckner, J. 2003. Strategic interaction among governments: an overview of empirical studies, *International Regional Science Review*, 26 (2): 175-188.

Bucovetsky, S. 1991. Asymmetric tax competition, *Journal of Urban Economics* 30 (2): 167-181.

Bucovetsky, S., and Wilson, J. 1991. Tax competition with two tax instruments, *Regional Science and Urban Economics* 21 (3): 333-350.

Chamley, C. 1986. Optimal taxation of capital income in general equilibrium with infinite lives, *Econometrica* 54 (3): 607-622.

Chari, V. V., and Kehoe, P. 1999, *Optimal fiscal and monetary policy*. In J. Taylor and M. Woodford (eds.), *Handbook of macroeconomics*, New York: Elsevier.

Checherita-Westphal, C., and Rother, P. 2011. The impact of government debt on growth. An empirical investigation for the Euro area, *Revue* économique 62 (6): 1015-1029.

Claeys, P., Moreno, R., and Surinach, J. 2012. Debt, interest rates, and integration of financial markets, *Economic Modelling* 29 (1) 49-58.

Conesa, J. C., Kitao, S., and Krueger, D. 2009. Taxing capital? Not a bad idea after all!, *American Economic Review* 99 (1): 25-48.

Devereux, M. P. 2004. Optimal tax rules for international portfolio and direct investment, *FinanzArchiv* 60 (1): 1-23.

Devereux, M. P. 2008. Taxation of outbound direct investment: Economic principles and tax policy considerations, *Oxford Review of Economic Policy* 24 (4): 698-719.

Devereux, M. P., Griffith, R., and Klemm, A. 2002. Corporate income tax reforms and international tax competition, *Economic Policy* 35 (17): 449-495.

Devereux, M. P., Lockwood, B., and Redoano, M. 2008. Do countries compete over corporate tax rates?, *Journal of Public Economics* 92 (5-6): 1210-1235.

Devereux, M. P., and Loretz S. 2008. The effects of EU formula apportionment on corporate tax revenues, *Fiscal Studies* 29 (1): 1-33.

Diamond, P. A., and Mirrlees, J. A. 1971. Optimal taxation and public production I: Production efficiency, *American Economic Review* 61 (1): 8-27.

Egert B., 2012, Fiscal policy reaction to the cycle in the OECD: Pro- or counter-cyclical? CESIFO Working Paper No. 3777, March 2012 https://ideas.repec.org/p/ces/ceswps/_3777.html

Eggert, W., and Goerke, L. 2004. Fiscal policy, economic integration and unemployment, *Journal of Economics* 82 (2): 137-167.

Eggert, W., and Schjelderup, G. 2003. Symmetric tax competition under formula apportionment, *Journal of Public Economic Theory* 5 (2): 439-446.

Eijffinger, S., and Wagner, W. 2002. Taxation if capital is not perfectly mobile: Tax competition versus tax exportation, EPRU Working Paper 2002-07.

Eurostat 2010. *Taxation trends in European Union. Data from the EU Member States, Iceland and Norway*. Taxation and Customs Union, Eurostat. http://ec.europa.eu/taxation_customs/resources/documents/taxation/gen_info/economic_analysis/tax_structures/2010/2010_full_text_en.pdf

Eurostat, 2014. *Taxation trends in European Union. Data from the EU Member States, Iceland and Norway*. Taxation and Customs Union, Eurostat. http://ec.europa.eu/taxation_customs/resources/documents/taxation/gen_info/economic_analysis/tax_structures/2014/report.pdf

Fernández, G. 2005. A note on tax competition in the presence of agglomeration economies, *Regional Science and Urban Economics* 35 (6): 837-847.

Fuest, C., Hemmelgarn, T., and Ramb, F. 2007. How would the introduction of an EU-Wide formula apportionment affect the distribution and size of the corporate tax base?: An analysis based on German multinationals, *International Tax and Public Finance* 14 (5): 605-626.

Garrett, G., and Mitchell, D. 2001. Globalization, government spending and taxation in the OECD, *European Journal of Political Research* 39 (2): 145-177.

Genschel, P., and Schwarz, P. 2011. State of the art. Tax competition: a literature review, *Socio-Economic Review* 9 (2): 339-370.

Golosov, M., Kocherlakota, N., and Tsyvinski, A. 2003. Optimal indirect and capital taxation, *Review of Economic Studies* 70 (3): 569-587.

Golosov, M., Tsyvinski, A., and Werning, I. 2006. New dynamic public finance: A user's guide, *NBER Macroeconomics Annual 2006* 21.

Gordon, R. H. 2000. *Taxation of capital income vs. labour income: An overview.* In S. Cnossen (ed.) *Taxing capital income in the European Union: Issues and options for reform*, Oxford: Oxford University Press.

Gordon, R. H., and Hines, J. 2002. International taxation, NBER Working Paper 8854.

Gordon, R. H., and Wilson, J. D. 1986. An examination of multijurisdictional corporate income taxation under formula apportionment, *Econometrica* 54 (6): 1357-1373.

Gordon, R. H., and Wilson, J. D. 2001. Expenditure competition, NBER Working Paper 8189.

Haufler, A., and Stähler, F. 2009. Tax competition in a simple model with heterogeneous firms: How larger markets reduce profit taxes, CESifo Working Paper 2867.

Haufler, A., and Wooton, I. 1999. Country size and tax competition for foreign direct investment, *Journal of Public Economics* 71 (1): 121-139.

Hellerstein, W., and McLure, C. 2004. The European commission's report on company income taxation: What the EU can learn from the experience of the US States, *International Tax and Public Finance* 11 (2): 199-220.

Houthakker, H.S, 1965, New evidence on demand elasticities, *Econometrica* 33, pp. 277-288

Huizinga, H. P., and Nielsen, S. B. 1997. Capital income and profit taxation with foreign ownership of firms, *Journal of International Economics* 42 (1-2): 149-165.

Judd, K. L. 1985. Redistributive taxation in a simple perfect foresight model, *Journal of Public Economics* 28 (1): 59-83.

Kapoor, M., Kelejian, H. H., Prucha, I. R. (2007), Panel data model with spatially correlated error components, *Journal of Econometrics*, 140, 1, 97-130.

Kind, H. J., Midelfart, K. H., and Schjelderup, G. 2005. Corporate tax systems, multinational enterprises and economic integration, *Journal of International Economics* 65 (2): 507-521.

Koskela, E., and Schöb, R. 2002. Optimal factor income taxation in the presence of unemployment, *Journal of Public Economic Theory* 4 (3): 387-404.

Krogstrup, S. 2004. A synthesis of recent developments in the theory of capital tax competition, EPRU Working Paper 2004-02.

Krogstrup, S. 2002. Public debt asymmetries: The effect on taxes and spending in the European Union, European Central Bank Working Paper 162.

Kuh, E., 1959, The validity of cross-sectionally estimated behaviour equations in time series applications, *Econometrica* 27, pp. 197-214

Kudła, J. 2013. *Ekonomia opodatkowania międzynarodowego*, Warszawa: Difin.

Kutarba, M. 2011. *Polska może stracić na wspólnej podstawie podatkowej*, http://www.obserwatorfinansowy.pl/forma/debata/polska-moze-stracic-na-wspolnej-podstawie-podatkowej/.

Lee, K. 1997. Tax competition with imperfectly mobile capital, *Journal of Urban Economics* 42 (2): 222-242.

LeSage, J., Pace, R. K. (2009), *Introduction to spatial econometrics*, CRC Press, Taylor and Francis Group, Boca Raton.

Ludema, R. D., and Wooton, I. 2000. Economic geography and the fiscal effects of regional integration, *Journal of International Economics* 52 (2): 331-357.

Mankiw, G. N, Weinzierl, M., and Yagan, D. 2009. Optimal taxation in theory and practice, *Journal of Economic Perspectives* 23 (4): 147-174.

Marceau, N., Mongrain, S., and Wilson, J. D. 2010. Why do most countries set high tax rates on capital?, *Journal of International Economics* 80 (2): 249-259.

Mendoza, E. G., and Tesar, L. L. 2005. Why hasn't tax competition triggered a race to the bottom? Some quantitative lessons from the EU, *Journal of Monetary Economics* 52 (1): 163-204.

Millo, G., and Piras, G. 2012. splm: Spatial panel data models in R, *Journal of Statistical Software* 47 (1): 1-38.

Mintz, J. 2004. Corporate tax harmonization in Europe: It's all about compliance, *International Tax and Public Finance* 11 (2): 221-234.

Mintz, J., and Weiner, J. M. 2003. *Exploring formula allocation for the European Union, International Tax and Public Finance* 10 (6): 695-711.

Mirrlees, J. A. 1971. An exploration in the theory of optimal income taxation, *Review of Economic Studies* 38 (2): 175-208.

Musgrave, P. B. 1972. International tax base division and the multinational corporation, *Public Finance* 27 (4): 394-413.

Mutti, J., and Grubert, H. 2004. Empirical asymmetries in foreign direct investment and taxation, *Journal of International Economics* 62 (2): 337-358.

Nielsen, S. B., Raimondos-Møller, P., and Schjelderup, G. 2010. Company taxation and tax spillovers: Separate accounting versus formula apportionment, *European Economic Review* 54 (1): 121-132.

Ottaviano, G. I. P., and van Ypersele, T. 2005. Market size and tax competition, *Journal of International Economics* 67 (1): 25-46.

Pebesma, E. J., and Bivand, R. S. 2005. Classes and methods for spatial data in R, *R News*, 5 (2): 9-13.

Pelster, M. 2014. Implication of financial transaction costs on real economy: A note, *Contemporary Economics* 8 (1): 113-118.

Peng, R. 2008. A method for visualizing multivariate time series data, *Journal of Statistical Software* 25 (1): 1-17.

Pethig, R., and Wagener, A. 2007. Profit tax competition and formula apportionment, *International Tax and Public Finance* (6): 631-655.

Piketty, T., and Saez, E. 2013. A theory of optimal capital taxation, *Econometrica* 81 (5): 1851-1886.

Pomerleau, K. 2014. A comparison of the tax burden on labor in the OECD, http://taxfoundation.org/article/comparison-tax-burden-labor-oecd.

Richter, W. F., and Schneider, K. 2001. Taxing mobile capital with labor market imperfections, *International Tax and Public Finance* 8 (3): 245-262.

Riedel, N., and Runkel, M. 2007. Company tax reform with a water's edge, *Journal of Public Economics* 91 (7–8): 1533-1554.

Romero, A. A., and Burkey, M. L. 2011. Debt overhang in the Eurozone: A spatial panel analysis, *The Review of Regional Studies* 41 (1): 49-63.

Rosen, H. S., and Gayer, T. (2008). *Public finance*, New York: McGraw-Hill.

Schäfer, D. 2012. The financial transaction tax – Boon or bane?, *Intereconomics* 47 (2): 76-103.

Shackelford, D., and Slemrod, J. 1998. The revenue consequences of using formula apportionment to calculate U.S. and foreign-source income: A firm-level analysis, *International Tax and Public Finance* 5 (1): 41-59.

Shinohara, M. 2014. Tax structure and economic growth, Institute of Economic Research Discussion Paper No. 217, Chuo University.

Sørensen, P. B. 2000. The case for international tax coordination reconsidered, *Economic Policy* 15 (31): 429-472.

Sørensen, P. B. 2004. Company tax reform in the European Union, *International Tax and Public Finance* 11 (1): 91-115.

Swank, D. 1998. Funding the welfare state: Globalization and the taxation of business in advanced market economies, *Political Studies* 46 (4): 671-692.

Szlęzak-Matusewicz, J. 2006. Reforma podatkowa w Unii Europejskiej, *Finanse publiczne*, Lublin: Wydawnictwo UMCS.

Tax by design, Oxford: Oxford University Press, 2011.

Tiebout, C. M. 1956. A pure theory of local expenditures, *Journal of Political Economy* 64 (5): 416-424.

Wei, T. 2013. *corrplot: Visualization of a correlation matrix*, R package version 0.73, http://CRAN.R-project.org/package=corrplot.

Wildasin, D. E. 2011. Fiscal competition for imperfectly-mobile labor and capital: A comparative dynamic analysis, *Journal of Public Economics* 95 (11-12): 1312-1321.

Wildasin, D. E. 2003. Fiscal competition in space and time, *Journal of Public Economics* 87 (11): 2571-2588.

Wildasin, D. E. 1988. Nash equilibria in models of fiscal competition, *Journal of Public Economics* 35 (2): 229-240.

Wilson, J. D. 1991. Tax competition with interregional differences in factor endowments, *Regional Science and Urban Economics* 21 (3): 423-451.

Winner, H. 2005. Has tax competition emerged in OECD countries? Evidence from panel data, *International Tax and Public Finance* 12 (5): 667-687.

Zodrow, G. R., and Mieszkowski, P. M. 1986. Pigou, Tiebout, property taxation, and the underprovision of public goods, *Journal of Urban Economics* 19 (3): 356-370.

Polish Studies in Economics

Edited by Ryszard Kokoszczyński

Volume 1 Wojciech Grabowski: Employee Stock Options, Payout Policy, and Stock Returns. Shareholders and Option Holders in Large U.S. Technology Corporations. 2012.

Volume 2 Jan Jakub Michałek / Michał Brzozowski / Andrzej Cieślik (eds.): The Relationship between Human Development, Exports and Foreign Direct Investments in Emerging Europe. 2013.

Volume 3 Tomasz Żylicz: The Economics of International Environmental Cooperation. 2015.

Volume 4 Juliusz Jabłecki / Ryszard Kokoszczynski / Paweł Sakowski / Robert Ślepaczuk / Piotr Wójcik: Volatility as an Asset Class. Obvious Benefits and Hidden Risks. 2015.

Volume 5 Janusz Kudła / Konrad Walczyk / Robert Kruszewski / Katarzyna Kopcewska / Agata Kocia: Modeling Fiscal Policy in the European Union. 2015.

www.peterlang.com

www.ingramcontent.com/pod-product-compliance
Ingram Content Group UK Ltd.
Pitfield, Milton Keynes, MK11 3LW, UK
UKHW021816051026
15470UKWH00026B/1393

9 783631 65830